THE CALM EFFECT

5 Keys For Introverts To Succeed
Without Stress and Lead With Poise

By Terrance Lee, MBA

PRAISE FOR *THE CALM EFFECT*

"The perfect follow-up to Quiet Voice, Fearless Leader. A must-read for introverts who want to strengthen their leadership skills while staying authentic to who they are." - **Matthew Pollard, award winning speaker and bestselling author of** *The Introvert's Edge* **series**

"Downright empowering...the best book I've read on how introverts can use calmness and become excellent leaders." - **Shanda Miller, bestselling author of** *From Supervisor To Superleader*

"In *The Calm Effect* Terrance Lee offers a heartfelt guide for introverts to thrive and lead with grace. With a personable approach, he shares his five keys to success, providing invaluable insights for leaders looking to navigate the world without stress. A must-read for anyone seeking to harness their introverted strengths and make a powerful impact!" - **Chelene Knight, author of** *Let It Go: Free Yourself From Old Beliefs and Find a New Path to Joy*

"Calm leadership is powerful leadership - and that's exactly the kind of leadership introverts are uniquely poised to offer. Gripping, inspiring, and empowering throughout, *The Calm Effect* shows introverts how to tap into their most underutilized strength and turn it into their biggest asset." - **Chelsey Brooke Cole, psychotherapist and bestselling author of** *If Only I'd Known! How to Outsmart Narcissists, Set Guilt-Free Boundaries, and Create Unshakeable Self-Worth*

The Calm Effect

First Edition Published April 2024

Copyright © 2024 by Lee Enterprise Group LLC

ISBN 979-8-9903108-1-0 (eBook)

ISBN 979-8-9903108-0-3 (paperback)

Cover Design by: Safeer Admed

Editor: Oluwadamilola Omotuyi

All Rights Reserved. No part of this publication may be reproduced, stored in a retrieval system, or transmitted in any form or by any means – electronic, mechanical, photocopy, recording, or otherwise - without prior permission of Lee Enterprise Group LLC.

I dedicate this book to my father John Daryl Lee,

my late grandfather Moses Pemberton Sr.,

and my late grandfather Fred Lee Sr.

I am here because of your faith, your sacrifice, your wisdom, and your prayers. Thank you.

As a bonus for buying my book, I'd like to give you a workbook for free! This workbook includes:

- **Summary of the core principles in each chapter**
- **Action plans for each principle**
- **Sections to take notes and personalize your action plan**

Scan below to download your copy:

CONTENTS

Introduction 1
Prologue 3

Part I - Poise 13
A Calm Voice 17
Dealing With Opposition 23
A Stable Temperament 29
Handling Pressure 33

Part Ii - Patience 37
Slow Down 43
Disconnect 47
Seek To Understand 51
Embrace Quiet 57

Part Iii - Observe 61
Pain Points 67
Body Language 71
Tone 75
Interactions 79

Part Iv - Connection 83
Listen Actively 87
Show Empathy 91
Establish Your Core Three 95
Acknowledge Other Perspectives 99

Part V - Relaxation 103
Unplug 109
A Great Team 113

Moments Of Solitude	117
You're Not In Control	121
Plan Of Action	123
Conclusion	125
Thank You	129
Acknowledgments	131
References	133

Calm

Adjective

A quiet and relaxed manner [1]

INTRODUCTION

As I stand in the kitchen and stare outside the sliding glass doors, I suddenly feel my heart racing, and my hands start shaking uncontrollably. I'm unable to move, momentarily paralyzed with fear. The brush behind our house is on fire. The fire's intensity grows by the second and gets closer. I sense that within a few minutes, my family's home is going to burn down.

PROLOGUE

FIRE IN THE DARKNESS

It's a warm summer night in Anaheim Hills, a suburb in southern California. Today is an ordinary evening like any other, where the flicker of streetlights signals us to leave from playing outside with our friends and head home. After eating dinner with my mom and sister, my dad arrives home after a long day of work and over an hour spent fighting through the Los Angeles rush hour traffic.

Beside our kitchen is a sliding glass door that leads to our backyard, which backs up to a small hill. Approximately one acre behind that hill is a mountainous area covered in plants and brush for what seems like miles. Some nights, I stare into the darkness through the closed glass door, watching as the wind blows the brush back and forth on the mountain, wondering what might be up there.

While playing together, my sister and I are startled by the screams of my mother:

"FIRE!! FIRE!!"

Immediately, we both run toward the kitchen in a panic and arrive at the glass door where my mother stands, looking shocked. Less than a mile away, we see a massive fire burning on the mountain behind our house. Brushfires are known to be a common occurrence in some areas of California, and on this night, it appears that one is headed right toward us. Realizing the growing danger, my mother begins running around the house frantically,

"Everyone, pack your bags, grab your clothes! Come on!!"

Breathing heavily, I run into my room and grab my T-shirts, pants, baseball cards, comic books, and other items to throw into a suitcase. After packing, I dread returning to the glass door to see how much closer the fire has come. During the chaos, a thought crosses my mind,

"Where is my dad?"

When he arrived home from work and we saw the fire, I hadn't heard anything from him. At that moment, I shift my focus to look for him, wondering why he wasn't scrambling to escape with us. Walking into the kitchen, I see a sight one might expect to see in a movie. With a direct line of sight to the approaching fire through the glass, my father is sitting at the kitchen table eating dinner. Upon first observation, he doesn't appear to be concerned or worried. He continues to eat while occasionally glancing through the glass at the fire that is gaining momentum toward our house and showing no signs of slowing down.

I have many questions to ask but find myself sitting next to him instead, not saying a word. I initially feel confused and scared as we both silently sit in the kitchen. But then a strange thing happens. For some reason, my fear slowly begins to calm. I'm unsure what is going through my head, but seeing his calm amidst the burning flames somehow settles me. I don't realize it, but after this day I will never be the same.

PROLOGUE

A CALM LEADER'S JOURNEY

Working in the fast-paced, challenging, and constantly changing Aerospace and Defense industry, a question that I often get is:

"Terrance, how are you so calm?"

For years, I didn't know how to answer this question. Reflecting now, I realize I grew up consistently seeing calmness under pressure through observing my dad. On the night of the fire, with everything in complete chaos, coming face to face with my worst fears as a 9-year-old kid, he didn't panic. That evening is just one example, but I could fill up a book with others. While watching the fire that night, we eventually heard helicopters flying over the area. We then saw large buckets of water pouring from multiple helicopters onto the mountain, slowly putting out portions of the fire until they had finally extinguished it.

Seeing his approach to this situation and so many others made me want to be the same way. I wanted to be that cool and at peace when everything around me would suggest I should be the opposite. Although I strived to model this throughout my life, I eventually wondered if my calmness was a strength or a crutch. Add to that my naturally introverted nature and an inner struggle where I began to question if my introversion would prevent me from achieving success. As a young professional, I rarely saw the laid-back, introverted person getting ahead. Employees who got promoted were typically outgoing, loud in meetings, and attended every social function the company offered. Meanwhile, my calm demeanor often led people to assume I lacked passion. And my desire to recharge as an introvert led some people to think I was antisocial.

Observing the career advancement of all my extroverted coworkers led me to believe it was time for a change. That change meant shifting away from who I was, so that's what I did. In group conversations at work, I talked even if I had nothing important to say. I started attending group outings after work, even if I was drained from socializing all week. I laughed at jokes I didn't find funny to fit into the group. After some time had passed, I looked up and began to wonder if I had lost myself. Before I knew it, my desire to be accepted and fit into an extroverted world had led to an increase in self-doubt and constant overthinking, and I was starting to feel like I might never be good enough. That was until I found another way, a better way, and never looked back.

In 2015, I accepted a new position as a project engineer for an extensive aircraft development program. This role was a significant step in my leadership journey, as our team consisted of over 50 engineers, and I was responsible for providing technical direction. What I remember the most about being in that role is not the number of aircraft we built and delivered to our customers or the fact that I had a title on an organizational chart. What I remember the most is that I decided to be myself. That meant no more pretending, no more acting like someone I wasn't, no more 'extroverting' to try and get ahead. I was going to be me, and that decision changed everything.

Today, if someone asks my secret to remain calm under pressure at work or in business, there is an answer. That secret is something that many successful leaders know. It can distinguish between someone constantly advancing their career or business goals versus someone who feels stuck. It is the difference between someone who can maintain healthy professional and personal relationships versus someone who always seems to turn people off. It is the difference between someone's ability to remain comfortable with who they are versus someone who is constantly insecure.

That secret is the calm effect.

INTENTIONAL CALMNESS

Can you relate to any of the scenarios or thoughts below:

- The people you see getting ahead are incredibly outgoing and take charge of conversations.
- To grow as a leader, you wonder if you must change your personality.
- Too often, you worry about what other people think about you.
- Sometimes, you overthink things that you've said or done.
- You wonder if being an introvert holds you back, a thought that sometimes leads you to self-doubt or stress.

I've been there and understand if you can identify with any of the feelings above. In the first book of the Introvert Leader series, *Quiet Voice Fearless Leader*, we focused on ten core leadership principles for introverts to have as a foundation. In this book, *The Calm Effect*, we focus on five secrets that will help you lean into a superpower that most people never experience: the power of intentional calmness.

Now, a question that I think is important for us to address is this:

Are all introverts naturally calm?

Some people might assume that the answer is yes. Externally, if someone is sitting in a room and appears relaxed or not as talkative, one might associate this behavior with calmness. However, this doesn't factor in what could be going through that person's head internally. Introverts can experience feelings of stress or anxiety that they may choose not to share with the outside world. For the record, extroverts can as well. At the same time, that person sitting in a room may be relaxed. Also, they may not be talking in a discussion because they're busy listening and absorbing information. So, while it may be tempting to assume all introverts are the same way, it's just not the case. The good news is that this book focuses on tools that will help you succeed regardless of where you'd consider your level of intentional calmness to be today.

INTROVERSION/EXTROVERSION – FACT VS. FICTION

As someone who has spent years researching and learning more about personality types, mainly focusing on the scale between introversion and extroversion, I've discovered many common misperceptions exist. For example, in a speaking engagement a few years ago where I spoke to a group of over 40 educators, I led them through an exercise where I asked the following:

What is the first word that comes to mind when you hear introvert?

Below is a collection of the most common responses that I received:

- Quiet
- Reserved
- Shy
- Laid-back
- Timid

When I asked the same question with the word extrovert, below were the most common responses:

- Confident
- Loud
- Outgoing
- Outspoken
- Assertive

Hearing this feedback, I wondered how those responses extrapolate to the larger population and how many others associate introverts and extroverts with those character traits. Ironically, it has become evident that most people in society have no idea what introvert and extrovert mean.

Swiss psychiatrist Carl Jung first popularized the use of introvert and extrovert in the early 1920s. According to Jung, an extrovert seeks intensive contact with the outside world. At the same time, introverts turn their psychic energy inward [2]. It has also been suggested that there are no absolute introverts or extroverts. Although most humans tend to lean more towards one direction than the other, leading to the classification of individuals as either introverts or extroverts, we ultimately all fall somewhere on the continuum between both extremes.

Unfortunately, many people don't associate introversion and assertiveness together. This inherent bias can affect whether or not someone gets promoted. It can become a factor in whether or not someone is viewed as a potentially good partner for a business deal. When thinking of an assertive leader, people often envision a louder-than-life personality who loves to be in the crowd. However, these people often miss that no data or research links introversion to a lack of assertiveness. There is a long list of well-known introverts who are fine asserting themselves in their fields. Some of them are among the wealthiest in the world, including the following billionaires:

- **Mark Zuckerberg (creator of Meta/formerly Facebook)**
- **Larry Page (co-founder of Google)**
- **Oprah Winfrey (media mogul, talk show legend)**
- **Bill Gates (founder of Microsoft)**

To name a few. But even with that in mind, a core truth about leadership often gets missed.

Often, the most influential leaders who can push a team to incredible heights and navigate a team through the lowest of lows, are the calmest people in the room.

LEADING WITH CALM

Some days, when I have a tight deadline to meet, a complicated presentation to prepare for, or a new challenge coming my way, I think about that night in the kitchen with my dad. I think about how enormous the fire was, how helpless I felt, and how all I could see was an outcome that would end in disaster. Today, maintaining a calm presence, which he modeled for me, has become necessary. There is always hope, even when faced with difficulties and circumstances that seem dire for my team. There is always a way out. That belief alone helps me stand firm and will help you stand strong too.

The ability to remain steady amid chaos lives inside of you. It's when life is throwing fire at us, and there seem to be obstacles in every direction that we turn. Our coworkers or business associates are all stressed beyond belief, worried, and wondering what to do next. The calm effect is an intangible power that allows us to sit amid a storm and be at peace. My hope for you is that through reading this book and applying each principle, you will begin to see your professional life, mindset, and relationships transform. You will no longer spend days and nights stressed out about your day or worried about your week. The obstacles in your path that seem impossible to scale will begin to fall. Problems that would have destroyed you before will become minute.

I do want to be clear here. I'm not suggesting that choosing the leverage of the calm effect means you will no longer have trouble. You won't always get it right. Operating in calmness is a daily journey that never ends. Sometimes I fall, and sometimes I'm not as steady as I should be. The point is always to get up, work to improve, and evolve. Just know that I am on this journey right with you. When others are loud, calm leaders are quietly planning their next move. While others are reactive when problems arise, calm leaders stare trouble in the face and calculate how to defeat it. You will find that operating with intentional calmness is the superpower you never knew you had.

PART I - POISE

"Success is largely a matter of adjusting oneself to the ever-varying and changing environments of life, in a spirit of harmony and poise."

~ Napolean Hill

On January 22, 1989, a man accomplished a heroic feat, with over 68% of all American households tuning in to watch him. Not only did he accomplish it, but his style, while doing so, created a legendary story. Superbowl XVI featured the San Francisco 49ers versus the Cincinnati Bengals. Late in the 4th quarter, the Bengals had secured a 16-13 lead in the game with a field goal. Following a penalty, the 49ers found themselves on their 8-yard line with 3 minutes and 10 seconds, or 104 seconds left to go in the game [3].

According to the story, in the game's climax, with 92 yards to go, an intense defense to battle against, over 39 million people watching at home, and thousands of people roaring in the stadium, this man responded to intense pressure in an interesting way. As he walked to the line, he turned to his tackle, Harris Barton, and casually remarked:

"Hey, isn't that John Candy?"

The story goes that Harris then looked over to the sidelines where the famous 1980s actor John Candy was eating popcorn. Harris acknowledged that it was him while sharing a moment of levity with his quarterback; the pressure and tension, at least for one moment, quickly subsided. Seconds later, the 49ers started their offensive drive, a historic string of plays that ended with them scoring the winning touchdown with 34 seconds left in the game, leading them to Superbowl victory in dramatic fashion [4]. The man in this story was named Joe Montana, and for his seemingly calm demeanor in moments of pressure, he became known by the nickname "Joe Cool." As an 8-year-old living in Northern California then, I'll never forget watching that game and celebrating our hometown team's win with my dad.

The Cambridge Dictionary defines the word poise in the following way:

Calm confidence in a person's way of behaving or a quality of grace [5]

How would you describe your natural demeanor? As you go through life, how do you generally feel? Please think and answer those two questions honestly. Lastly, what do you think other people would say about you? One thing about life we learn as adults is that 'adulting' is not always what it's cracked up to be. There are some difficult days at work, disappointments in business, and struggles that occur in our relationships. On the other hand, there are times when everything is great, life seems to be flowing on autopilot, and we have no worries at the forefront of our minds. When we're down, it feels like the sky is falling and there's no way out; when we're up, it feels like nothing could go wrong, and it will last forever.

The truth is that contentment is the key to reducing the stress that comes with our troubling times and managing the emotions that come with our wins. Think about someone you know who appears to be content. Notice I didn't say someone who seems to be 'happy,' as happiness can fluctuate daily. There's a poise, a balance, and a calm confidence that some people have, and you can naturally feel. This first secret of the calm effect is critical as a foundation. Imagine the next time you hear bad news about a project at work or the next time a situation threatens to shut down your business. Instead of reacting out of worry or starting to overthink, you find yourself feeling a sense of peace and resolve. It's not that you believe everything is perfect, but you find yourself exhibiting a level of poise and calm that you can't explain. The tools for how to attain that level of composure and apply it directly to your career or business as an introvert are what we'll be covering in this section of the book. You and I may not be Superbowl quarterbacks, but we can operate with a level of poise that other people admire and respect.

A CALM VOICE

"A calm voice simply means communication centered on logic, reason, and respect."

The relationship between sound and the human brain is intriguing. In an article titled "The Science of Sound," Dr. Sol Marghzar explores how our brain's limbic system controls our behavior and emotional responses. In particular, he notes that the amygdala is sensitive to sound, the primary reason humans react emotionally to things we hear. Dr. Marghzar states that our emotions can become attached to certain sounds based on our past experiences; therefore, hearing certain sounds can provoke various thoughts and behaviors [6].

Reflecting on my youth, particularly between the ages of 13 and 14, I can recall moments of rejection when asking a girl I liked for her phone number. In those instances, sad ballets like Boyz II Men's "End Of The Road" or Jodeci's "Cry For You" would play in my head, and I immediately felt sorrow. My overthinking would kick in, and I started pondering why she might have rejected me, leading me down a rabbit hole of thoughts throughout the rest of the day.

However, I also remember growing up in a house where my mother frequently played the relaxing tunes of smooth R&B, jazz, and gospel music. I recall the upbeat conversations and the laughter as our family bonded and enjoyed each other's company. What we consume and feed into our brains directly impacts us; the same applies to communication. Have you ever spent time around a group of people and begun imitating their speech patterns or mannerisms? You may have relatives in a particular part of the country with specific slang local to their region. Within a few months of living around them, you'll more than likely, without even knowing it, begin to pick up their dialect casually. People who study new languages will probably tell you that one of the best ways to learn a new language is to spend time in a country that speaks that language. Or what about someone's mood? Have you ever been around someone who consistently talks about people, is often disgruntled, and complains a lot? Depending on which people you are around more often, you may pick up some of their habits. Now, knowing that, here's the cool part. If you ever want to change the energy in a room, if you ever feel like the vibe is off or there's tension building in the air, you have the power to change and shift it. And that shift starts with something straightforward, a calming voice.

Picture this scenario. A team of engineers just got news from their supply chain leader about a shipment that was supposed to arrive today. The shipment is being delayed by three weeks. This shipping delay will cause the program to be late delivering products to their customer, making this news terrible and unexpected. The team wants to tell their project manager about the problem, but there's just one issue. The project manager is known around the office for having a temper and not taking bad news well. The last time anyone came to him with news of a schedule slip, they were yelled at, told to fix it, and embarrassed in front of their team. So, you can imagine how the engineers on this team feel about telling their manager about the slip. Fearing backlash, they keep the news to themselves instead of letting the manager know. They choose to work directly with the supply chain team and correct the issue without the manager finding out. A day goes by, then a week passes, and the shipment delay still needs to be resolved. In addition to that, nobody has brought it up to any leadership. In a meeting, the project manager asks nonchalantly:

"So, how's that shipment coming? We should have received those parts last week, right?"

An uncomfortable silence fills the room, the engineering team looking at each other to see who will speak first. It finally comes out that the supplier's shipment had been delayed, and worse, the team had known about it for over a week. It's not a good situation all the way around.

So, who's ultimately to blame in this situation? The team for not letting their manager know about the issue or the manager? Although the team should have communicated the news as soon as they were made aware, their leader did not foster an environment where everyone felt safe sharing. Their leader should have valued being a calm voice. For the record, I am not suggesting that a calm voice means having a softer or reserved tone, although it could depend on your communication style. I'm also not saying that having a calm voice somehow means being a pushover or someone who will never challenge anyone. A calm voice means communication centered on logic, reason, and respect.

A perfect example is a program manager, Corrina, whom I worked with. Corrina's personality is outgoing and vibrant. As someone who worked with her during some extremely tense situations with what seemed like impossible deadlines, I found that while her gregarious personality was apparent, so was her calmness. The cadence of her speech was typically very fast-paced. Picture someone who speaks a mile a minute, rapidly firing off thoughts, suggestions, and questions. But while many people do this, what separated Corrina was that when she spoke, it was clear to everyone that she knew what she was talking about. She had confidence and a calmness that would naturally put our team at ease.

In *Quiet Voice Fearless Leader*, we stated that the team takes on the personality of its leader. When a leader is high-strung or erratic, that will be the tone throughout the rest of the organization. When a leader is thoughtful and calculated, that will also set the tone for the organization. So always remember this: your calm voice can completely change the culture of any environment for the better.

PLAN OF ACTION

Breath Control – when tension is high, or we begin to feel nervous, it can cause any number of physical reactions to occur. Our palms can get sweaty, our hearts can beat fast, or our feet might start to tap nervously. Naturally, when we feel this way, our cadence of speech can be affected. We may begin to talk faster than usual, stumble over our words, or forget what we must say. To relax your voice, pause for 5 to 10 seconds and breathe in and out. Repeat this exercise until you begin to feel your nerves calm. Over time, you will start adapting and learning to do this exercise without thinking about it, allowing you to communicate with a calming voice.

Practice Speaking Calmly – nothing beats practice and repetition when learning a new skill. The next time you're speaking to someone at work, speaking to a business associate, or a loved one, pay close attention to your voice. What does your normal tone sound like? As an experiment, monitor your speaking habits over the upcoming week and note what you notice. Now, the week after that initial observation, commit to being intentional about calm communication and cadence when you speak. Try it out and see what happens; you might be surprised at the difference.

Know Your Information – I've found that sometimes people who talk fast and appear erratic in their behavior are being that way because they're trying to hide something. I picture the used car salesman who knows he's about to sell you a lemon that will break down within a year. Or the time-share representative trying to convince you to purchase one of their packages (which you'll never be able to sell). When you're comfortable and confident in a subject, you will naturally communicate it efficiently. So, studying and mastering your skillset is a direct way to ensure you can speak calmly.

DEALING WITH OPPOSITION

"When you lose your cool, you give other people the power."

In 2009, President Barack Obama gave his State of the Union address to members of Congress in Washington, D.C. Historically, the State of the Union covers several controversial topics that the American public is either divided on or feels very passionate about. At one point in his speech, President Obama discussed one of the more controversial issues, the American healthcare system. After making a statement regarding his new health care plan, house representative from South Carolina Joe Wilson yelled out:

"You Lie!" [7]

A collective gasp was heard throughout the congress chambers. Not only did this happen with the entire world watching, but it was directed at the nation's President. After hearing the remark, President Obama raised his hand and pointed a finger toward the congressman, indicating that he heard what was said. Then, in a moment when tension and emotion in the room were extremely high, President Obama continued with his speech. Not only did he continue speaking, but his tone and cadence appeared unchanged and unbothered.

I want to be clear that this example has nothing to do with Democrats, Republicans, and whose political parties are right or wrong. It transcends political affiliations; this is simply a case study of human behavior. Depending on your perspective, you could take this interaction in one or two different ways. One person would think:

"Wow, he's just going to let himself get disrespected like that with the world watching? If that were me, I would've yelled back! What a coward."

Another person would think:

"What poise and class for him to handle it that way. That he could continue his speech without pause made that congressman look foolish."

Regardless of which perspective you believe to be accurate or your political beliefs, most of us would agree that President Obama displayed admirable restraint and self-control in that situation.

In science, the law of conservation of energy states that energy is neither created nor destroyed, just transferred from one form of energy to the next [8]. If President Obama had yelled back at Congressman Wilson and they had engaged in a shouting match live on national television, what would he have gained? In that scenario, Barack would've allowed Congressman Wilson's emotional reaction to transfer to him.

How often do we inadvertently allow this to happen? Have you ever had a great day where everything is going fine, and someone begins complaining about the weather and how it is too hot or cold? If you have, you know that the next thing that happens is you start to think about the same thing, which puts a damper on your mood and puts you in a different headspace. We often see this with school bullies. Children who bully others are usually not powerful, although they may appear so to the child being bullied. Typically, they're pretty insecure. A study conducted by researchers from the University of Washington and Indiana University discovered a direct connection between children exposed to intimate partner violence at home and bullying. Of the children studied, 97% of the bullies stated they were also victims of bullying [9]. The reality is that many bullies are desperately trying to transfer the negative energy that they receive at home or elsewhere to someone else. There is a phrase that says, "Hurt people hurt people." This statement has proven to be accurate.

Part of carrying ourselves with poise lies in practicing discipline and self-control. Trust me, I get it; this is hard! Situations will happen where we feel wronged. We feel taken advantage of, misunderstood, unheard, and like the other person should pay. For introverts who typically feel and think deeply, these scenarios can sometimes cause us to dwell on the details of everything that happened.

This principle does not mean avoiding standing up for yourself. In fact, in a later chapter, we'll be addressing how to handle conflict while maintaining your self-control. So, how do you prepare for the moment somebody comes at you? The moment at work, in business, or your personal life when it's clear that someone is either being condescending, disrespectful, or opposing you in some way? Here are some tips to remember.

PLAN OF ACTION

Eyes On The Mission – during intense moments, it's vital that we're able to distinguish our emotions from our mission. In the State of the Union example, President Obama's emotions at the moment might have said:

"This guy just yelled at me and is trying to embarrass me in front of the world. Who does he think he is?!"

That simple thought would lead many people to an abrupt reaction. Although it might feel good in the short term, that reaction can damage your reputation and peace of mind. The question you must ask yourself is, is the payback worth it? At that moment, Barack was focused on his mission. A mission that said no matter what distractions came, he would deliver an important speech that had the power to either tear down or strengthen the faith of the American people. When we begin to live our lives focused on a mission that is bigger than just us, we will naturally make wiser decisions regarding our emotions.

The Power Dynamic - here's a phrase that my 8-year-old and 6-year-old will often say when they are in the middle of a sibling dispute:

"She made me mad!!"

"He made me upset!!"

My wife and I quickly correct our children and remind them that no one can **make** you lose your temper. When we lose our self-control and composure, not only is that a choice, but we are completely giving away our power. Allowing the person opposing you to drive you toward an emotional response turns you into a puppet. With any disparaging remark or action, if you get emotional, you give them power, and they hold the puppet strings. When you are challenged and remain intentional about keeping your same energy, the power dynamic swings in your favor. So remember, be the puppet master, not the puppet.

Keep Your Tone - reflect briefly on the definition we read for energy conservation. Now, picture yourself in a meeting where someone's tone with you gets out of control. They say something that upsets you to your core, and you fight to hold back your tongue. If you respond with the same elevated voice they had, then you are now matching their energy. However, if your tone during the discussion has been your regular cadence of speech and you respond that way, you have effectively maintained control of the conversation. Ironically, this might frustrate the person as some try to beat you into stooping down to their level. But when you keep your tone and don't waver from who you are, that's where your strength lies.

A STABLE TEMPERAMENT

DEFINITION OF TEMPERAMENT

CHARACTERISTIC OR HABITUAL INCLINATION OR MODE OF EMOTIONAL RESPONSE

People who often lose their control or their composure can quickly turn people off. One disruptive or damaging experience, even two, may be tolerable. But when someone begins to show a pattern of lacking self-control or a pattern of lacking essential character traits, it begins to get old very fast. Conversely, when someone shows themselves to be a person who can be calm regardless of the situation and assertive while remaining respectful, that person is more likely to attract others to them.

Despite what some people may think, a person's general temperament is not static and can change over time. Factors like significant life-altering experiences or intentional adjustments in behavior can cause a person's personality or temperament to change. This change goes for both introverts and extroverts. I see my story as an example of this.

As an outgoing and expressive person, I enjoyed talking and being around people. However, a traumatic incident in the 7th grade, detailed in the introduction of *Quiet Voice Fearless Leader*, led me to go inward. For years, this journey included everything from self-silencing, to self-doubt, to depression, to feeling misunderstood, to feeling alone, and a range of other emotions. My loud demeanor was replaced with something else: a kid who was afraid, doubtful, ashamed, and pretending to be something I wasn't. It was not until I learned the truth of what I was, an introvert, and what that meant that I began to understand so much about myself. Suddenly, so many things made sense. I felt drained when hanging out around crowds for extended periods. I always felt closer connections to people talking one-on-one instead of in groups, and I loved in-depth conversations instead of small talk. It all began to make sense. The best part is that I began to embrace it. My introversion, which was once a crutch, became my superpower. With all that said, one's temperament can change, and having a stable demeanor becomes critical to win with the calm effect.

A person's day-to-day temperament can have a significant impact on a team. To illustrate that point, I'd like to tell a quick story about two different leaders. Both are people I've worked with on prior programs, and both were in high levels of leadership at the companies I worked at. I'll avoid using real names for this example, so let's call the first leader Bob and the second leader Leo.

Bob was an intense guy. When he communicated, he would do so with passion, or what many people perceived as such. But for some reason, Bob always just seemed to be on edge. We had a very demanding customer then, and the product we were working on was experiencing several technical issues. Problems continued to surface over time, so I noticed a few things about Bob. In meetings, upon hearing news of a failure from an engineer, Bob's immediate response was visible frustration. His responses to the engineers typically appeared accusatory or very direct. It reached the point where many meetings would end without discussing problems or addressing solutions, leaving the engineering team needing clarification. Bob's habit of leaving meetings early, visibly flustered, became a regular occurrence. If you passed him in the hallway, you would likely get a very reluctant head nod, rarely a good morning or good afternoon, followed by conversation. Working on Bob's team was not a calming feeling. Other engineers on the team frequently voiced their desire to work under other program managers; some were even worried that he might try to get them fired.

Now, let's contrast that with Leo. Leo joined our team on a high-profile, highly complex aircraft prototyping program. The scope of his contract was four times the size of Bob's, but honestly, I never saw Leo stressed. Don't get me wrong. I know he had bad days because our team had bad days. This was the first aircraft of its kind, and anyone with a technical background knows that your first time doing anything will not go without incident or issue. However, Leo's approach when problems arose differed significantly from Bob's. When an issue came up, it was typical for Leo to call a meeting and bring the team of engineers into a room for a collaborative working session. I called the meetings collaborative because that's what they were. Although he was the leader in the room and typically helped lead the discussion, it was always a discussion where everybody was heard. Leo's temperament seemed to always remain steady even when describing complex issues to our demanding customer, a customer unwilling to budge on our delivery requirements or schedule. Consequently, you rarely heard engineers talk about wanting to leave Leo's team; when someone new joined our program, Leo became known as one of the leaders you wanted to work for.

So, how do you ensure people view you in the same light as Leo instead of Bob? A lot of it starts with having a stable temperament. Can you maintain composure whether times are good or bad? This is the difference between a reactionary leader who allows life's events to push them around versus a poised leader who stands firm in what and who they are.

PLAN OF ACTION

Observe winning behaviors – do you work around anyone that you admire? Most of us have a person we look up to or a mentor. If you have anyone like that in your life, then I want you to study them. Watch how they interact with other people, watch how they react after making a mistake, watch how they respond to failure. Watching and learning from the winning behaviors of others gives you an advantage. Most of us attempt to win by gaining wisdom from our own experiences and taking the time to learn from the experiences of others.

Observe losing behaviors – that's right, just as important as modeling yourself after someone you view in high regard is essential, it's equally important to learn from people who are the opposite of what you want to become. I would even argue that you might retain more by watching someone setting a bad example than a good one. It gives you the blueprint for exactly what not to do. When you see a leader that's running their team in a way where you say:

"Wow.... what are they thinking?"

It would help if you took note of that. Keep a stable temperament, learn something new daily, and never allow that to be you.

HANDLING PRESSURE

"Poise and confidence are a natural result of proper preparation" – John Wooden (former UCLA basketball coach, 1948-1975).

As a high school basketball player, my free-throw shooting skills were, to put it lightly, not incredible. I was terrible at it. For those reading this unfamiliar with basketball, statistically, anyone shooting around 80% or above is considered an excellent free-throw shooter. It could be better if you're about 65%, but it's decent. My free-throw shooting percentage my senior season was closer to 53%, so yeah, it was terrible.

One night, we were playing our rival Plano East, who had beaten us earlier in the year on our home court. On this night, we were the away team playing in their gym in front of a loud and rowdy crowd. The game went back and forth the entire night. It was an intense matchup where the winner would be in a good position going into the state playoffs. Late in the fourth quarter, with less than 30 seconds remaining, we were down by two points and had possession of the ball with a chance to tie or win. I caught a pass from my teammate and drove toward the basket, where, in the process, instead of getting a shot off, I was fouled. This meant I would now go to the free-throw line and had to make both shots to send the game into overtime.

Our coach called a timeout, and we began walking toward the bench. The walk felt like it was in slow motion. I could hear the roar of the crowd, could feel my heart pulsing and my hands beginning to sweat. Of all things, why did it have to be free throws?? The energy in the huddle was tense, each of us sitting there looking at Coach Hicks and waiting for his guidance. He looked at me, seemingly ignoring everyone else in the huddle, including the opposing cheers from the sideline behind our bench.

He then said something that I'll never forget:

"<u>When</u> Terry Lee hits both free throws, we'll get into this defensive formation. And get a stop."

Although the pressure of that moment felt insane, and a district title was on the line, Coach Hicks saying that changed something. When we got up from the huddle and began walking toward the free-throw line, I had extra confidence in my walk. For some reason, I felt loose; the crowd screamed, but I was able to block it out. I walked to the line and, just as Coach Hicks predicted, hit both free throws in a row. After a defensive stop, we carried that momentum into overtime and were able to walk away with a win that night.

The point of me bringing up this story is much bigger than a 40-plus-year-old man reliving his high school glory days - although I must admit it felt good to do that - the broader point is that Coach Hicks taught me something that night that has helped me to remain calm in higher pressure situations for years. He taught me the power of visualization.

Pressure can cause us to feel several different emotions, from the weight of expectations to self-imposed standards. The feeling that if we don't perform up to a certain level, then we will let somebody down or maybe even let down an entire team. There's also the pressure that we put on ourselves. It's when no one is putting pressure on us, but we hold ourselves to a certain standard in our minds. If anything falls below that standard, we need to improve. I can identify with both as someone who has spent most of my life battling perfectionism.

Throughout your life, you will run into situations where a lot is at stake, and the pressure is on you to fix it, especially if you're a leader. The truth is circumstances will not always be in your favor, and you must navigate through them. In these moments, choosing calmness over worry can carry you through. So, what do you do when the pressure is on? When you're in the heat of a big moment, when you have a significant deadline, when you must execute, when you're nervous or scared, visualize yourself performing at the highest level.

What do you usually visualize in big moments? Some of us might envision the worst-case scenario; after all, several things could go wrong. But at that very moment, you want to do the exact opposite. When you have a big presentation for work, instead of worrying about how it will go, why not visualize yourself acing it? Everyone who hears you will be confident that you know your subject matter and are the right person to speak. The great thing about gaining experience is that over time, the more situations where you face pressure and overcome, the more your confidence and ability will continue to grow. Instinctively, when you get into a difficult situation, you'll remember the last time you were in one and overcame it.

PLAN OF ACTION

Embrace the moment - when you have a big meeting to lead, when you and your team receive some bad news, when your day starts excellent, and halfway through it, when you're ready to throw in the towel, those are the moments that you must embrace. Yes, that might sound counterintuitive.

But what's the alternative? Our only other options are to run from the problem or ignore it. The issue with those approaches is that they only make things worse. Instead, please assess what's happened and consider a plan to fix it. Embrace what's happening and decide to fight it.

Don't take work too seriously - if a doctor told you that you had one week to live, what would be the first thought that comes to your mind? Chances are, it would have little to do with your career or your business. For me, I want to spend as much time with my family and close friends as possible; that's all I want to do. This may be an extreme example, but life is short. You will have some days that suck. You will have some other days when everything is fantastic. When the pressure is on, it's important to remember not to take yourself too seriously. Whatever work you do, I encourage you to be fully dedicated to performing at your highest level. Yes, it would help if you worked to accomplish any goals or milestones you've set for yourself. But at the end of the day, our work is not life or death. Remember that when you're under pressure, smile, laugh it off, accept your situation for what it is, and always keep pushing forward.

PART II - PATIENCE

"To lose patience is to lose the battle."
~Mahatma Gandhi

In the Fall of 1962, the world was on the brink of nuclear war. For over 13 days, the United States and the Soviet Union engaged in a dangerous military standoff that had the potential to turn catastrophic and alter the course of human history forever. Previously, the United States had attempted to overthrow Cuban leader Fidel Castro in the Bay of Pigs invasion. After the invasion, the United States received intelligence that Soviet Union leader Nikita Khrushchev had reached an agreement with Castro to place Soviet nuclear weapon sites in Cuba to prevent any future invasions from the United States. As the following days played out, in an event now known as the Cuban missile crisis, tensions grew high. Missile sites continued construction in Cuba, less than 90 miles from the United States coast. President Kennedy issued a public warning against any offensive weapons in Cuba; meanwhile, construction of the nuclear sites continued. Many of President Kennedy's advisors at the time encouraged an aggressive approach. A strong recommendation from his Joint Chiefs of Staff included an air strike in Cuba that would have been followed by an invasion, a move that would have been an explicit declaration of war. With a threat this real, with close advisors advocating for such an approach, many leaders would have proceeded with the air strikes. However, Kennedy chose a different route. Instead of reacting aggressively, he communicated directly with Khrushchev, held press conferences informing the American people about the growing situation, and sent U.S. Naval Forces to set up quarantine lines to prevent Soviet ships from arriving in Cuba with offensive weapons. As the world watched, the fate of millions of lives at stake, both leaders and their advisers engaged in a military chess match that seemed only to be progressing in the wrong direction. Surprisingly, on October 28th, 1962, Khrushchev issued a public statement that the nuclear sites in Cuba would be dismantled, essentially leading to an end to the crisis [10].

I always like to think about what if. When President Kennedy first got word of the missiles in Cuba, things could've played out very differently. Let's assume for a minute that he'd taken the initial advice of his advisors and invaded Cuba again. There is a strong chance that this decision could've led to nuclear war, a decision that once acted on could not be reversed. But instead of acting off of initial instinct or emotion, President Kennedy paused, weighed the options, and ended up choosing a path that eventually led to a peaceful resolution. When we choose to act off emotion, there can be dangerous consequences. When we learn to pause and think first, the outcome can be very different.

Our society is the most impatient that it's ever been. Waiting has become a foreign concept, a luxury few are willing to indulge in. When I was growing up, we had our favorite television shows that would come on every week. We would eagerly anticipate the day our favorite show was scheduled to air. Since then, the live television model has changed drastically. With the multitude of streaming platforms, from Netflix to Hulu, Disney, and many others, why would I wait for a television show to come on one night during the week? In a consumer's mind, why watch that show for 2 to 3 months when a streaming subscription will allow someone to binge-watch an entire season of episodes in two days?

I remember spending many Saturdays with my parents, running errands and shopping. Many times, those errands would take most of the day. Now I watch as, in a matter of 5 minutes, my wife has browsed the Internet and managed to order all our groceries while also buying multiple items from Amazon that will magically appear on our doorstep within 24 hours. Insert into this equation the rise of technologies such as artificial intelligence. As of this writing, a massive surge of AI applications allow people to do everything from creating marketing campaigns, hiring virtual assistants, writing books, and countless other tasks. We are, in fact, the most impatient that we've ever been. This impatience is why what I'm about to say will likely be unpopular to many, but a few may understand.

Technology has undoubtedly advanced our society; innovations allow us to accomplish tasks in fractions of the time that it took 20 to 30 years ago. While that is great in theory, it does come at a cost. That cost is our increased impatience.

So, what's the harm in that? Well, for one, when you're impatient, you miss things. In the middle of our cutting-edge technology, fast-paced society, and hectic schedules, we often need to remember a crucial principle. And that is the principle of patience.

Simply put, most people don't take the time to pause and think anymore. There often never seems to be time for that in our world. We rush, make quick decisions, move forward with things that we may not be ready for, and ultimately, that leads to a series of events that spiral out of control. It can lead to bad decisions, which, from a business and corporate sense, can have negative consequences for your company or your business. A mentor once told me that doing things right the first time is always more effective. If not, the amount of money and time you'll spend on rework will make the project much less productive. If you are an introvert reading this, there is good news. Due to your naturally introspective nature, this principle will likely be easier for you to adopt. Many introverts, including myself, prefer to think before speaking as often we want to process our thoughts first. There are many benefits to this way of thinking, and in this portion of the book, we'll be exploring several ways that you can leverage this to your advantage.

As you learn to apply the principle of patience, you'll notice its calming effect on you and other people you work with. Instead of a frantic environment where thoughts are scattered and everyone speaks on a whim, conversations will begin to become more meaningful, filled with thought and strategy. Imagine an environment where everyone calmly voices their opinions and thinks before speaking. This is what can happen when we learn to pause.

SLOW DOWN

"How many disagreements, fights, even wars might have been prevented by one person who chose to stop and think for just a few seconds."

Have you ever said or done something that you immediately regret? While playing basketball in the fifth grade, I went through a period where referees frequently called technical fouls on me during games. It usually happened when I missed a wide-open shot, or a referee made a call I disagreed with. In those instances, my immediate reaction would be to slam the ball on the hardwood in frustration. The referee would blow the whistle, call a technical foul, and my coach would take me out of the game.

What causes incidents such as fits of road rage or heated exchanges between two coworkers to occur? Often, these situations are triggered when an incident causes a person to lose their self-control. Once that incident occurs, there's a small window where anger can overcome logic. Logic would say to that person that although this happened to me, it's not worth losing my cool and doing something foolish. However, anger and frustration are emotions that overcome many people and cause them to act out. People often say or do things without thinking in a work or business environment.

An example is when a person is put on the spot in a meeting and asked about something to which they don't know the answer. At that moment, many people address the question with a response they know may not be correct. In that person's mind, the alternative is not answering and coming off as someone who doesn't know their information. Unfortunately, this mentality often backfires, leaving the person who responds quickly to come off as unprepared and unsure.

The ability to slow down can prevent us from encountering issues in many situations. The concept is quite simple: in moments where you begin to feel emotions of anger, confusion, frustration, or doubt, slow down and pause before speaking or acting out. Again, if you're an introvert reading this and consider yourself an inward thinker, implementing this approach may be straightforward. People who function this way tend to think first and then follow that thinking with words. The other approach is for people who talk to think, where they prefer speaking first and figuring out the answers as they talk. Which of these communication styles describes you? It's not that one approach is necessarily right and the other is wrong, but it is essential to understand what comes naturally to you.

I enjoy observing different presentation styles, whether through a webinar or a talk online, an in-person conference, or a group meeting. One thing that I pay close attention to is how the person presenting handles answering questions. When asked a question, many presenters quickly fire off a response. As soon as the question leaves someone's lips in the audience, they are already talking, at times before the other person has even gotten their whole question out. And for some people, this approach works. It is, however, obvious when that person is responding quickly to respond, and the reality is that they may or may not have fully understood the question.

Let's try a quick exercise. The next time you talk to a coworker, friend, family member, or significant other when they ask you a question, I want you to contemplate what they asked and not say anything for at least five seconds. Now I get it; 5 seconds may not seem like a long time, but for someone not used to pausing, those 5 seconds of complete silence can feel like an eternity! Ultimately, slowing down allows you time to do the following:

1. Assess the question

2. Acknowledge any emotions that you may be feeling.

3. Consider the right approach and proceed.

Imagine a world where more people took time to slow down instead of reacting to their first instinct or carnal emotion. How many disagreements, fights, and even wars might have been prevented by one person who chose to stop and think for just a few seconds?

PLAN OF ACTION

Weigh the cost - I am all for respectful disagreement, emphasis on the word **respectful.** Disagreement is necessary and beneficial when two people can't get on the same page. However, when the debate is carried out without thought and done distastefully, what can it cause? Sometimes, it can lead to someone not wanting to work with you or a bad working relationship. So, when a comment is made that you don't like or disagree with, be sure to weigh the cost of any reaction you may have.

Wait five seconds – Some people are sitting in a jail cell over a decision made within a few seconds. Example – a twenty-something-year-old man is out drinking at a bar, and someone bumps into him. After bumping into him, the person makes a rude or disrespectful comment, ensuring he can hear it. In that moment, reacting to emotion, the twenty-something-year-old attacks the person. The next thing he knows, a full-blown altercation ensues, and the police are called. The night ends with the twenty-something-year-old getting booked and locked up at the local jail. It happens all the time, but now, let's translate that to a corporate or business environment. Someone feels like they are just not being heard. In a split second, they decide to go off on their coworker. So, they do it, and the result is damage to their reputation, damage to their brand, and immense damage to their relationship with that coworker. At the height of each of these moments, with tension and anger at an all-time high, what if each of these people waited five seconds before doing anything? Slowing down and waiting can ease the nerves and allow rational thought to flow. So don't rush, just wait.

DISCONNECT

"Learning how to be still, to be still and let life happen - that stillness becomes a radiance" – *Morgan Freeman*

In an article published by People magazine, research suggests that the average U.S. adult will spend the equivalent of 44 years staring at screens [11]. That includes everything from typing away on a work computer to checking text messages to scrolling through social media. Outside of that, consider someone with a significant other or someone with children. For that person, when time is not spent working, watching television, or enjoying some other form of entertainment, their time is typically spent running errands, driving kids to school, or doing extracurricular activities.

Life is a series of constant movements for many people, especially working adults, from when they wake to sleep.

One activity needs to be added to most people's daily agenda. That activity is stillness. A few years ago, my business coach, Dr. Lawana Gladney, had me do an exercise where I wrote out every activity in my day over a week in 30-minute increments. At the time, I felt extremely overwhelmed and couldn't understand why.

As someone with a wife, two children, a demanding career, a growing author brand, and a ministry leader at church, among other things, I struggled with figuring out how to balance everything.

The first time I reviewed the daily tracker with her, I was amazed at what I saw. What I saw was a life with no pause. No wonder I felt overwhelmed and barely had time to catch my breath. While the exercise was somewhat discouraging initially, it opened my eyes to opportunity. I began to see times in the day when I could get a task completed in 15 minutes instead of 30. I started to see specific tasks that were just busy work, which ultimately wasn't moving the needle in my life. It was time for things like that to go.

Think about how often you're able to be still. Not by accident, not when you're bored, not due to some outside force. But how often are you **intentionally** still?

Stillness might look different for different people. Stillness can be achieved through prayer, meditation, yoga, sitting under a tree, looking at a lake for 10 minutes, or walking in the park. Whatever it is for you, stillness and calmness go hand in hand.

Truthfully, you can even practice stillness amid a stressful or chaotic situation. When we begin to feel our anxiety rising, it can have many detrimental impacts on our mindset and our health. In those moments, try to pause and figure out a time to break away.

You may be in the middle of a call or sitting in a meeting, so you can't get away right then. But when you find the opportunity, pause and disconnect, even if it's just for a few minutes. Take that time to be still in the best way for you. You'll find that you will undoubtedly feel refreshed when you reengage with your work.

If you're a busy career professional or entrepreneur, trust me, I know it's hard. Some days, it may feel like you barely have time to breathe. Amid that, for introverts, disconnecting to some degree becomes even more critical after spending an entire day socializing virtually or in person. Even if it just means having a few moments to think.

Plan Of Action

Stop worrying about your emails – FOMO or fear of missing out is real. People fear missing out on the right investment opportunity, missing out on a trip to a new hot vacation destination, and missing out when it comes to their work. It's the feeling of being worried that you will miss an important message that requires your attention immediately if you are not checking your emails. If you worry about the potential message you won't see because you've chosen to disconnect, I want you to hear this.

Work is always going to be there. And despite what you may think, you don't have to be the person to do it all. If you know you need to step away for some time alone, delegate someone else to do your work while you're away. Don't allow yourself to be controlled by FOMO.

Find a stopping point - to meet tight deadlines on high-visibility projects throughout my career, I have regularly worked late into the night or sometimes early before sunrise. As I examined this work pattern, I realized that some extra work wasn't even necessary. Sometimes, you can find yourself at a place where you're working on tasks just to be working, thinking that you're making progress when, in reality, your level of productivity has decreased.

Think about it: what was the urgent rush for you to cut back on your sleep, miss out on time with your family, or miss out on much-needed recharging to complete a few 15-minute tasks?

In many cases, tasks like these could have waited until tomorrow. When we find ourselves here, we need to ask if getting those things done at the expense of our work-life balance was worth it. Try to find a stopping point every day when you declare that you've officially switched from work to leisure mode. Anything that you still need to get done by that point in the day can become priority #1 later.

SEEK TO UNDERSTAND

DEFINITION OF UNDERSTANDING

THE CAPACITY FOR RATIONAL THOUGHT OR INFERENCE [12]

In many human interactions, we communicate but do not understand each other. Let's take the example of a married couple having the same argument for over ten years. Whenever an issue arises, they discuss it and leave the room believing they've arrived at a solution. Life goes on, a few months pass, and the argument comes up again. The offended partner continually feels like their partner just doesn't get it. Why do the same argument and the same issue continue? The cycle continues because although they talk about it, they may not understand each other.

Or take a group of coworkers who have been trying to solve the same problem on their project for over a year. Each person offers an opinion on what they believe should be done; they even decide to hire an outside consultant to help. When the consultant starts working with the team, sitting in on meetings and reviewing the project's current state, they discover something. The problem that this team has been trying to solve is the wrong one. The team thought they understood the issue that needed to be fixed, but in reality, they had spent an entire year pursuing an incorrect approach.

The truth about understanding is that it often requires patience. For the couple in the above example, part of their problem may be giving up too quickly on the conversation. What if they discuss their issue every time it comes up, but only at a surface level? They talk about it for 10 to 15 minutes and continue their day. But they might need over an hour and a half of painful, gut-wrenching, truthful conversation to arrive at a real solution. Something that both might be avoiding. Or, with the example of the team, they might have been feeling additional pressure to solve the problem on their project quickly due to company deadlines. Unfortunately, as a result, they rushed and missed some critical details. Had they paused to understand more about the problem they were solving, then a lot of time could have been saved. Taking the time to seek understanding upfront is essential to getting things done effectively, avoiding wasted time, and ensuring focus in the right areas.

When conversations are flowing rapidly, ideas are tossed back and forth, and to an observer watching, it may appear as if everyone is on the same page. This often happens in fast-paced work or business environments. Take the example of John and his manager, Rob. In the weekly team meeting one afternoon, Rob says to John:

"Okay, John, so by next week, can you have that document sent to me? That would be great."

John nods his head in agreement and says:

"Yep, no problem. I'll have that right to you."

The following week, John emails the document over to Rob.

Within a few minutes, Rob calls John into his office, and to John's surprise, Rob says:

"I'm sorry, John; I know you worked hard on this, but this isn't what I expected." Rob then tells John about all the adjustments he needs to make to the document. John nods and agrees to make the changes, but internally, he is frustrated.

He spent long days at the office trying to get this done and is starting to feel unappreciated. This outcome could have likely been avoided if both John and Rob had paused during the initial meeting and considered a few factors:

- Did John understand the detailed task being asked to complete?

- Did Rob communicate the specifics to John about what he expected to see in the document when it was delivered?

These scenarios play out all the time; it often happens when people are not taking the time to pause and understand what someone is saying to them.

The good news is that straightforward solutions can significantly reduce the chance of this occurring.

Plan Of Action

Repeat For understanding – This concept is one that was mentioned in *Quiet Voice Fearless Leader*, and I feel it deserves to be highlighted again. I learned a trick from my dad several years ago without realizing I was learning it. Over time, I noticed a particular pattern in many of his conversations. Somebody would say something to him, and he would respond with the following:

"So, what I believe you're saying is..."

He would then repeat what he believed the person meant. Sometimes, the person would respond by affirming that what he took away from the comment was correct, while other times, the person would explain that they meant something else. He explained that repeating what you believe someone said helps prevent confusion and misunderstanding. Since implementing this practice of repeating for understanding, I will tell you that countless hours, even days, have been saved on various projects I've worked on. The cost of someone walking away from a conversation without a clear understanding can be expensive, which is a way to keep that from happening.

Answer The Question - I can usually tell when one of our children isn't listening; it's when my wife or I are talking, and our son's eyes wander around the room. Or when we're talking, our daughter is busy looking at her favorite doll.

Within a few seconds of speaking, one of us will ask them to repeat what we just said. Suddenly, they raise their head, looking directly at us like a deer in headlights, and nine times out of ten will repeat something that is nothing like what we said. That said, I'm not writing this to single out my children because you and I do it too.

When someone is talking and asks you a question, it's essential to take in what they're asking entirely. To fully understand what they're asking, it's important to listen so that you can decipher what they're asking you.

Admit You Don't Understand - During many conversations, people will throw out ideas or ask questions to gauge the room and see who agrees or disagrees with them. When this happens, most people will naturally respond by nodding yes, as if they understand what the person is saying. However, inside, they may feel unsure about what was said. It can become a herd mentality, where everyone else in the room is nodding their head in agreement, and to avoid the risk of being singled out, some people will go with the flow and nod their heads, too. But this is very dangerous. As described before, we risk leaving the conversation needing more clarity about what's going on when we do this. This only leads to wasted time, miscommunication, and frustration between teammates. So, when you feel like you lack understanding, it is perfectly okay and wise to admit it.

EMBRACE QUIET

"Viewing silence as productive, powerful, and refreshing instead of awkward will completely transform our human interactions."

There are a lot of things that make people uncomfortable. Examples are long lines at the grocery store, sitting in rush-hour traffic, missing a connecting flight at an airport, or an air conditioning unit that goes out in your car in the middle of summer. Another one that many people rarely talk about is awkward silence. You know those moments in a conversation where two people are talking, and at some point, one has just run out of things to say?

This moment is bizarre for many people, so the instinct is to say something to fill the void. In broadcasting, this silence is known as dead air, the thought being that a conversation should constantly be flowing back and forth between two parties. Most people even go out of their way to avoid silence when they're by themselves.

While at home, they turn on the television to make noise in the background, even though they may not be watching it. Or, while driving, people will turn on music, their favorite podcast, or other forms of entertainment to consume. Anything to avoid quiet.

However, a dynamic should be considered here. For introspective introverts who like to think before speaking, sometimes awkward silence will happen. In fact, for many introverts, these moments of silence are not awkward at all, and the good news is that it's perfectly okay. The ability to not feel pressured to speak when there's nothing to say is rare.

And the ability to pause and sit in moments of silence can be used to one's advantage. When some people are trying to get to know someone for the first time, they might ask an icebreaker question like the following:

"So, where are you from? What do you do for a living?"

For one person, that question triggers a quick response that includes details about their upbringing, parents, and various experiences.

However, another person hearing that question may take a deep breath, look to the sky, and reflect on their adolescent years. After five to ten seconds, that person responds with their answer. When I am often asked a question in a meeting, particularly a question requiring a decision, I rarely fire off a quick reply. Usually, the question sparks my brain to think in different directions, considering various options and potential courses of action.

In the past, I wondered if this trait was something that I needed to change about myself. I would ask myself questions like:

"I wonder if people think I'm slow, or think I'm not following the conversation, or I'm confused."

After all, throughout my career, many leaders I've observed often address questions quickly. The truth is that the approach works for some people; if your natural communication style is to respond rapidly during conversations, then there is nothing wrong with that. But if you're reading this and your natural tendency is to think before speaking, you should realize there's nothing wrong with that approach. When we take the time to pause and embrace silence during our conversations, it does two things:

1. **It prevents our words from sounding rushed, incomplete, or inconclusive.**

2. **It increases our ability to add genuine input and value to the conversation.**

What I eventually learned is what I want you to take away from this chapter. When you view silence as productive, powerful, and refreshing instead of awkward, then it will completely transform your human interactions.

Plan Of Action

Forget what other people might think about you - as introverts, we can overthink at times (all my fellow overthinkers raise your hand high!). If you've ever gone silent in a room full of people, you may have had the following thoughts cross your mind at some point:

"I wonder if that person thinks I'm upset since I'm not talking."

"I wonder if they think I don't know what I'm doing. The other people here are so much more talkative than me."

Regardless of the thoughts that may cross our minds, we can do nothing to influence other people's thoughts. Since we cannot control another person's thoughts, we shouldn't worry about them. If you need to take a few seconds to think before speaking, then pause and do it.

Formulate a response - when asked a question, instead of responding rapidly, it's okay to take a few seconds to think about your answer, in particular, if you're not 100% sure of what you want to say. Use these seconds to do one of two things:

1. Form a response to the question or

2. Prepare to respond by saying, "I will have to get back to you on that one; I will take action to get you that answer."

Either of these approaches is perfectly fine and is a valid response.

PART III - OBSERVE

"The power of accurate observation is commonly called cynicism by those who haven't got it" ~George Bernard Shaw

From the time we are young, it is in our nature to be observant. An infant is at the complete mercy of their parents, unable to eat or move around independently. But that infant hears and absorbs their surroundings' voice, behaviors, and environment daily. As a toddler, children begin to pick up on language and increase their motor skills primarily through observing the words and movements of other people. By the time a child is ready to start school, their mind has become increasingly curious.

They ask about everything, from why the sky has clouds to why the grass is green, and the dreaded question, where do babies come from (I haven't got that one yet from my kids, but it's coming). Children are naturally curious and long to learn more about their world. But for many of us, this childlike curiosity can disappear as we age.

In a world full of distractions, work, and daily responsibilities, many people miss what's happening around them. Like a son who has been asking his dad to play a board game for weeks and the dad (while looking down at his phone) responds:

"Sure, son, let me get some work done first, then I'll come play with you".

The dad might be missing the disappointment and rejection on his son's face at that moment.

Or the person that's in the middle of making a point during a discussion at work, and their coworker cuts them off a few seconds into them talking and says:

"You know, I was thinking something a little different.... why don't we go this other direction?"

That person doesn't see how their coworker now feels unheard and unimportant. They attempted to express a critical thought, which was completely stepped on.

In a fast-paced world, moments like these happen all the time. The good news for those who intentionally observe people and their environment is that there's a distinct advantage. The advantage is that you'll be able to see, hear, and feel things other people are missing. For many introverts, there is a natural ability to do this exceptionally well. As deep thinkers, while everyone else in the room is busy talking, the introvert often observes and takes everything in. Even while talking, we can typically pick up on several cues that provide important insight.

While others are blind to the nuances and minute details around them, you can learn to observe them and act.

For a minute, let's picture the following scenarios:

Scenario #1 - you've been hired for a new job and are eager to start.

It's a role you've wanted for years, so you are excited about the opportunity. You want to get a few words in and contribute to the conversation in the first meetings you attend. In your mind, this will ensure you make an excellent first impression and prove that the company made the right choice in hiring you. Due to this self-imposed pressure to speak up, you decide to say something at the next staff meeting, even if you don't have anything to say.

Scenario #2 — you have decided to branch out and start a new business. This has been your dream for years, and you can't wait to get it off the ground. To ensure a smooth start, you have assembled a team of hardworking people to work with. However, because it's your business, you feel like there's an expectation for you to be the one who creates and implements most of the company's ideas. As a result, you work tirelessly to accomplish several tasks, even though you have people beside you who could do them.

Scenario #3 - when meeting new people in hopes of making a professional connection, you feel the urge to impress them. After all, your outspoken extrovert counterparts always talk about the new people they met, had lunch with, or exchanged contacts with.

You feel like being an introvert keeps you from experiencing the same results. So, you approach new conversations as if you have something to prove, to prove that you can talk, be more outgoing, and be memorable, even if it means breaking away from your true self.

You are not alone if you have encountered one of the scenarios above or experienced something similar. The societal pressure to excel, to stand out, and even to conform can impact our actions and behaviors. However, I suggest a different approach. The first thing you want to do when you find yourself in a room with new people, on a call with people you work with, in a discussion with a potential new client, or whatever the situation may be, is to observe.

Being observant means returning to your inner child when you were curious about people, your surroundings, and in a constant state of learning.

When working on a team, it is essential to have varying perspectives, and the perspective of someone who sees what everyone else is missing becomes very important. The ability to effectively observe also goes hand in hand with calmness and awareness.

And when you can pick up on what's happening around you, you'll be fully aware of your current reality and everything that comes with it.

So how do you use observation, or the art of reading the room, to benefit you and those you work with? In this section of the book we will focus on learning to observe five key things.

These apply to any environment, whether you are new to a group or have worked with the same people for years. It works whether the environment you are operating in is thriving or the climate is experiencing significant difficulty.

It takes a level of calm and confidence to sit back and observe. Nobody else will know you're doing it; truthfully, they don't need to know. When you become a master observer, the insights you gain can be life changing.

PAIN POINTS

"The more problems you solve, the more successful you and others around you will be."

One day, my parents, sister, and I envisioned a multimillion-dollar idea at the dinner table. At the time, we kept losing the remote control for the television. Usually, it had ended up in someone's room, behind a chair, or lodged deep in a couch cushion. I can't recall who expressed the idea first, but it was like a lightbulb went off:

"Hey.... what if there was a device that could find your remote control when you lose it?"

Immediately, we started brainstorming. We discussed what the device would need to do, the number of people it could help, and its potential to grow. It was a fun conversation. We left the dinner table that evening and didn't discuss the idea in detail again; the year was 1996.

Fast forward to several years later. The first patent for a remote-control finder was filed in the United States in 2000 and was granted in 2003. If you look up remote control finders online today, countless device variations are available. The point of that story is that four people sitting around a dinner table identified a problem. There was a specific pain point that we saw and wanted to address. Now granted, we didn't act on the idea; I don't believe that any of us knew how to implement something like that at the time. But

I learned from that experience to constantly observe and look for ways to solve problems.

Any good business venture is all about solving a problem. Electric vehicle companies like Tesla are creating cars that save people money on gas, are better for the environment, and feature state-of-the-art technology. Disneyworld realizes that parents who work all year long and kids who are in school look forward to a break. At Disneyworld, a family gets to break away from their routine, enjoy rides, take pictures with Disney characters, and watch fireworks. Like any company fills a gap and provides a solution to someone's pain point, you and I can do the same thing.

When you talk to people you work with, do you identify their problems? Are you hearing them when they express their concerns? If we pay attention to people when they're talking, there will be cries for help occasionally. Unfortunately, it is easy for us to miss when this happens entirely. Other times, the cries can be blatantly obvious.

For example, your coworker has been working on the same task for several weeks and has yet to be able to make progress. Every time you talk to them about it, they sound stressed. Not only is the project late, but your coworkers have realized that they may need to learn how to do it. Well, the task they're working on is within your area of expertise. You could pick up on one of their struggles by simply listening to them and offering assistance.

Don't get me wrong; I'm not saying you need to offer to do everyone else's work for them. That can become crippling for the other person, as they may never learn how to do their job without help. But when you see a need and are in a position to meet the need, then jump in and assist where you can. The more problems you solve, the more successful you and others around you will be.

PART III - OBSERVE

PLAN OF ACTION

How can you help? - No matter how well-run a team seems, something must always be fixed or improved. As an introvert, this is where you can lean into your natural ability to listen and absorb (which we'll be covering in-depth later in the book). Most people love to talk about their problems, whether the problem is professional or personal. When someone starts talking about a particular issue they're going through, please sit back, pay attention, and listen as they share it.

During these conversations, try to identify at least one area you or someone you know can help them with.

Find a quick win - in football, the quarterback has several options on any given play. The exciting plays for the crowd watching are when the quarterback drops back, throws the ball 50 yards downfield, and a receiver catches it for a touchdown. Another option, although less exciting, is when a quarterback throws and completes several 5- to 8-yard back-to-back passes. Eventually, if done consistently, the team will drive the ball to the goal line and score. It ends up being the same result but implemented in small increments. That's how we should help people. Many of us will hear a person's problem and want to help them solve it immediately. But what are some small things that we can help them with today? What's one thing we can do for that person that can be a quick win? Look for those opportunities first.

BODY LANGUAGE

"55% of communication is nonverbal, 38% is vocal, and 7% is words" ~ Albert Mehrabian, body language researcher [13]

I had the pleasure of interviewing a body language expert last year for a podcast. In the interview, my guest, Janette Ghedotte, explained that our ability to read body language is an unspoken human ability that has been forgotten by most of society.

She described in detail what it means when someone responds to a question you asked by shrugging both of their shoulders versus just shrugging one. Or when you're giving a presentation at work, and someone sitting at the table has their feet pointed toward the door instead of pointed in your direction. In Janette's mind, entire conversations occur through body language when people sit together.

She even told the infamous story of Alex Murdaugh, a man who was sent to prison in South Carolina for murdering his wife and son, a sad and twisted case made famous by the Netflix documentary "Murdaugh Murders." In one scene of the documentary, Alex Murdaugh is in court, appearing to get emotional with the judge and jurors watching. You see him squeezing his eyes together with his fingers in what appeared to be a sentimental moment in the courtroom as he reflected on the death of his family. According to Janette, her observation of his body language indicated that he was grasping at his tear ducts, a motion that can be done when a person wants to force him or herself to cry. When she told me that, it completely changed my view of that scene, from a man seeking genuine sympathy from a jury of his peers to a man who was quite possibly a narcissistic psychopath. Observing, reading, and genuinely understanding body language helps us understand what is happening around us at a deeper level.

According to body language researcher Albert Mehrabian, 55% of communication is nonverbal, 38% is vocal, and 7% is words, a concept known as the 55/38/7 formula. If we're observant, we can often sense how another person is feeling without them having to say a word. Consider the husband who comes home from work and asks his wife how she's doing. Looking away from him, with folded arms and a slight scowl, she responds quietly with:

"I'm fine."

Her words said that she was doing okay. But her body language should tell her husband that she is not only not okay, but she's also mad! Something is wrong, and that husband will probably spend the evening trying to get to the bottom of it. Or with my wife when I start explaining a "new idea" that I just came up with, but it's something she suggested to me months ago. As I'm talking, she'll be listening with a slight smirk. She won't interrupt or say a word; instead, she'll sit there with the "I told you so" look.

Now, translate this into the corporate or business environment. As a leader, when conversing with my team, I'm constantly watching for all the things that are not being said. When I bring up a controversial idea that will challenge our usual way of handling business daily, I want to see if anyone's arms are folded. I'm looking for scowls or smug looks on faces. These are just a few expressions that typically indicate resistance or disagreement. Or when someone makes a point, and one of their coworkers grasps their eyes as if trying to settle down a migraine headache. This gesture is typically a clear indication of frustration.

Life can get incredibly hectic between balancing a career, a family, a social life, and various issues. With all of that, focusing on other people's body language may sometimes seem like an afterthought. However, the person who notices it and can adjust based on what they see is extremely powerful.

PLAN OF ACTION

Listen and watch — listening intently to someone when they're talking is extremely important. But watching a person's movements, gestures, and facial expressions is equally essential. You may discover that although someone communicates one thing through their words, their body language may indicate something completely different. Pay close attention to non-verbal cues, whether in a meeting, a one-on-one discussion, or watching someone present on a topic.

Take notes and adjust — once you've observed someone's body language, it's time to take note of it and adapt your communication style as necessary. For example, you're briefing your leadership on the progress of a project you're working on. At one point during the brief, you talk about a very complex portion of the project. When you finish speaking, you look around the room, and although no one is saying anything, you can tell that a few appear confused. At that moment, you can ask a question like:

"So, did that make sense to everyone?" or

"Any questions or feedback about what I presented here?"

If anyone has a question or needs help with what you said, they will typically say something to you. And that's exactly what you want to happen. If everyone truly understands what you have communicated, then it's possible that silence means everyone is on the same page, which is a good outcome as well.

TONE

"It's not what you say; it's how you say it."

I've always found it interesting how somebody can say something, and the person who hears it can misinterpret what they heard. A mother asks her son:

"Hey, did you do your homework?"

or that mother can ask the same question but with an elevated pitch that sounds accusatory:

"Hey! Did you do your homework???"

A woman asks her coworker:

"Do you think you'll have that report done today?"

but feeling pressure from her management to complete the task on time, she asks the same thing but with a hint of sarcasm and condescension:

"So....do you think you'll have that report done today?

There are two areas to observe when it comes to tone. We need to observe our own, and we need to observe the tone of other people.

When it comes to us, as with most things, there is the way we believe we come across, and there is the way we do.

Picture a frustrated manager trying to get status from someone on his team for a few weeks. In a team meeting with other people present, he says:

"John, what's going on with this project?"

Here's the thing: One question can be expressed in several different ways. If that manager is already under pressure or on edge about the subject, then there is a strong chance that could come out in his tone. If the question is asked condescendingly or dismissively, then John will undoubtedly feel targeted and may even feel embarrassed. It's not a recipe for a healthy work environment.

However, the manager can ask the same question, just in a different way.

"So, John, how's the project going?"

Although the manager is under an extremely tight deadline, you wouldn't be able to tell by his tone because he sounds calm and is just seeking information. John now feels comfortable to open up and talk about the challenges he's been having with the project and his recent progress. The good thing is that as John was talking, the manager realized there were several areas where he could help him finish the project faster. The meeting ends with them taking a few actions to save the company precious time and money, ultimately a win-win scenario for all parties. But they only got to this point because the manager checked his tone.

At some point, you may have worked with or been around people who appeared to be completely tone-deaf or naturally came off as combative. An excellent exercise to try is recording yourself during intense conversations. You can use your phone, or record conversations that occur virtually to capture as much discussion as possible.

When the day is over, replay the recording and listen to yourself and others who were talking. What you hear may surprise you. You may pick up on points in the conversation where your voice inflection is raised or when someone comments and another person replies in a way that many would consider rude. Try this practice for a few weeks and begin noticing patterns. You may notice there are specific things that people do or say that often work your nerves. Or maybe after listening and noticing another person's tone, you realize that person only addresses a few team members with respect while others are talked down to. Over time, the more you key in and observe tonality, the more you will notice things others may never see. After all, it's not what you say; it's how you say it.

Plan Of Action

Listen for frustration – As a kid, I learned what happens when you shake a bottle of soda hard and open it. After getting a Sprite from the convenience store, I would immediately start shaking it; once I was far from anyone else, I would twist the bottlecap. At that moment, soda would begin overflowing and spraying out of the bottle. This happened because the shaking caused pressure within the bottle; once the lid was opened, all that pressure was released and came out as soda flying everywhere. If we're not careful, the same thing can happen with our emotions.

When people are frustrated and the time comes to talk about it, it can pour out confusion, anger, disappointment, and other feelings. As you listen to someone speak, pick up on any signs of this early in the conversation. Do your best to understand the source of where they're coming from and how you can help them.

Listen for joy - Equally important as observing the frustration in someone's tone is identifying when someone is joyful. For example, you have an idea you want to present to your team for the first time. There's one person who is usually cynical and objects to most of the new ideas that people present to him. So, you already go into the meeting expecting him to question your words. Surprisingly, you finish your presentation, and in an upbeat tone, he says:

"Interesting, I never thought of this approach. This could be a game changer for us."

Not only did he reply positively, but based on his tone, you could tell he was happy with your work. When you hear this type of response to something that you said or did, take note of it. It's an indicator that you're on the right track.

INTERACTIONS

"When the energy in a room is positive, you feel it; when it is bad, you feel that too."

Have you ever been in a room where you could tell that two people didn't care for each other? Neither one of them explicitly said to the other person:

"Hey, for the record, I don't like you and would prefer not to work with you."

But without any words, there was something about the energy in the room that you could feel. Their interaction led you to believe that an underlying issue existed.

Or you've been a part of a group discussion where someone is speaking, and another person interrupts them to begin expressing their thought instead. At that moment, you may have looked over at the person who had just been interrupted and caught a look of disgust on their face. On the other hand, you may have been in a work or business environment where you could tell that everyone in the room had a mutual respect for one another. Without saying it, the room's energy suggested that everyone there felt appreciated and heard. These are two vastly different rooms. The power comes when we're able to observe all interactions and navigate both environments.

The observation of human energy is a fascinating thing. You cannot reach out and feel or even explain it to someone else. When the energy in a room is positive, you feel it; when it is bad, you feel that too. In an interview with my friend Audra Russell for her 'Between The Reads' podcast, she told me the story of an event she attended with her daughter. Throughout the event, her introverted daughter did not say much and spent more time people-watching. She said that when they left and got in the car to head home, her daughter gave her the full play-by-play of who in the room liked each other and who had issues with each other. I would imagine that other people at that event had no idea she could observe their every move. This unspoken gift and ability to read the room is something that many introverts can naturally do.

This gives you a critical edge, and there are steps that you can take to leverage it. One important use of this ability is in conflict resolution. When you find yourself or people that you work with engulfed in conflict, there is a three step process to follow.

Acknowledge The Disagreement - when observing an interaction between two individuals you work with, you notice that they often disagree when talking to each other. When speaking to other coworkers, they are incredibly polite and open, but for some reason, when speaking to one other, each of them gives off an energy that is combative and cold. If you were oblivious to this, you could completely miss a freight train that could impact you and your team. When you have observed enough interactions to see an issue between two people, you know there is something to address. It could be that someone recently got a promotion the other person was passed up for. The person who was passed up must come to work every day feeling like they should be in their coworker's position. Or it could be that they feel threatened by each other. During discussions, especially in groups, each is eager to prove their points and appear more knowledgeable than the other person.

Whatever the issue, once you observe it, it's time to address it.

Seek Clarity - First, you want to start by gaining clarity on the situation, which starts by conversing with each person individually. While talking, ask both the same question:

"So, I've noticed in recent meetings there is tension between you and (insert name). Am I off there?"

You don't want to make anyone feel accused or called out, so phrasing this as a question instead of an accusation is vital here. After that, your job is to sit back and listen, simply giving them the space to prove you wrong or share their truth with you. Next, if they respond confirming that they do have an issue with the other individual, then say:

"Understand, and I appreciate you sharing that with me. So how do you feel that we can rectify the situation?"

After asking this, allow them to speak and take note of their response. In most situations, there is a tangible solution that will work for both parties involved.

Resolution - Once a solution is identified, the final step is to converse with both people in the same room or on the same call. This step is critical to this process; you don't want anyone to operate off gossip, and you want everyone to be on the same page. Meet with both people and start with the solution as the focus of the discussion. Allow them to air out any grievances they have, to vent, but ultimately have everyone walk away with the solution in mind.

Plan Of Action

Be neutral – working in the kids' ministry at my church; I have to be careful when kids approach me with an issue they're having with another kid at church. They're coming to tell me their version of a story, their version of an incident. I already know that, most likely, the other kid will tell me something completely different. It's the same way in the corporate or business environment. Being able to observe interactions effectively means being able to remain neutral anytime two parties are having an issue without taking sides. By doing this, you ensure your ability to be impartial regardless of what appears to be happening around you.

Keep the peace – let's face it, people are emotional. The emotional state of many human beings can change from day to day; for some, it changes hourly. We shouldn't attempt to force people to be anything other than what they are; after all, most people will continue to operate similarly. What we can do, though, is attempt to keep the peace.

Someone who keeps the peace knows how to squash unproductive conflict, how to see when conversations are going in a negative direction, and how to advise others on how to push toward a positive outcome.

PART IV - CONNECTION

"Surround yourself with people who are going to lift you higher" ~Oprah Winfrey

In 2004, a movie titled 'The Butterfly Effect' was released. In this film, starring Ashton Kutcher as the main character, he frequently experiences traumatic headaches that cause him to lose consciousness.

While in this state, he can travel back in time and alter reality. Throughout the movie, while visiting the past, he makes several choices that lead to a different future outcome for himself and others. Sometimes, the alternate future reality is better than his current circumstance. Conversely, in one scenario, his past actions create a new reality where he is imprisoned. It was a brilliant movie highlighting how our choices can impact our lives forever.

The principle of the Butterfly Effect also holds in our relationships with people. Our ability to relate, understand, and connect with people can change our future reality forever. Also, how we speak to others, how they talk to us, and how we handle and approach situations with our peers and colleagues can have lasting effects.

If you're an introvert reading this, I want you to know something important. A lot of commentary, videos, and posts on social media would lead you to believe that introverts want nothing to do with people.

Somehow, the word introvert is often falsely tied to being a social recluse, unable to connect or bond with others. This belief could not be further from the truth. Introverts can relate and create meaningful relationships quite well due to our natural ability to listen and tendency not to require the spotlight.

Throughout my life, I can recall several instances where two people used to be best friends, and a disagreement, a misunderstanding, or a fight caused them never to speak again. It can happen when a family member brings up a dark memory from the past to someone at a family reunion; words are exchanged, and someone says something they can never take back. It could be two people working together daily while having a tense relationship.

One day, their conversation crosses a line from healthy debate to being condescending toward one another. Once that line is crossed, the lines of communication are challenging to repair and may never be. Now, depending on your natural temperament and your communication style, you could be thinking:

"Well, that's just how I am; I'm straightforward and honest. I'm going to tell you how I feel."

Growing up in the 80s and 90s, in the golden era of action movies, my generation clearly understood what we **believed** strength to be. In the era where megastars such as Arnold Schwarzenegger, Sylvester Stallone, Bruce Willis, and others reigned, the stereotypical alpha male was front and center.

These movie stars would win every fight, dodge every bullet, and ultimately save the day. A genre that raised many of us to believe that strength meant a domineering, take-no-prisoners attitude.

In legendary sports rivalries of that time, such as the Detroit Pistons versus the Chicago Bulls and the Los Angeles Lakers versus the Boston Celtics, games were physical, and no love was lost. These matchups occurred at a time when a player could dribble the ball toward the basket attempting to dunk and find themselves catching an elbow to the face, getting hit in the ribs, or worse, and the referee might blow the whistle. It was an era when my favorite baseball pitcher, Nolan Ryan, got in a historic fight. During one game, after Nolan threw a wild pitch, a batter charged the mound to fight Nolan. When the batter dove toward him, Ryan put him in a chokehold and began mercilessly hitting the top of his head. I remember my friends and I talking about that fight after it happened and reenacting it.

Many of us looked to the examples above as models for how to deal with our anger. And for some of us, that initial instinct to fight, battle, and argue stuck and never left. Unfortunately, when we approach human interaction this way, it often does more damage to us than it does to anyone else.

Now, I want to be clear in saying that there is nothing wrong with direct communication and with being upfront when you speak.

As someone who has worked in the Aerospace and Defense industry on US government contracts for almost 20 years, direct communication is what I'm used to. That said, there can come a point where we're so focused on making our point, being right, or trying to be what we perceive as strong that we are no longer relating to anyone. When we're no longer relating, we forget about the human connection that is vital for any team or organization to succeed.

In this section, we will learn how to connect to people on a deeper level. The ability to connect is a highly valuable skillset that delivers benefits beyond the workplace or business world. Imagine being able to truly understand and engage with others in a way that you never have before. You will begin to walk with a calm confidence as you notice the level of trust and respect between yourself and others continues to grow.

LISTEN ACTIVELY

"A person talking without hearing anyone else is just having a one-sided conversation."

I'll be honest: I love a good debate. It's something that my friends and I used to do nonstop in high school and college. We would debate everything from our favorite sports teams, which song was better, and who had the better hometown. Anything could become the debate of the day. In its essence, there's nothing wrong with debate, and there's nothing wrong with disagreement. Both can be done respectfully and can even be healthy things to do. However, many people need to pay more attention to an essential aspect of debate: the art of listening.

You see, there's no debate without active listening. A person talking without hearing anyone else is just having a one-sided conversation. The reason that many people don't listen is simple. Most of us are selfish. We have a thought we'd like to express, and we become so determined for the other person to hear us that we completely forget what they might think. This happens constantly in the workplace, the business world, and our personal lives.

While some people enjoy being in the spotlight, being the first person to be called on in a room or the first to speak up, the introvert may not. As a consequence, the introvert is typically a naturally good listener. People long to be heard and to be understood. Who better to do that than the person who is okay with being slow to speak, the reflective person who wants to hear and understand? Lean into your natural ability to listen and watch your relationships transform.

Okay, confession time. My wife knows I can't do anything else if she needs to talk to me about a subject that requires my attention. I'm a horrible multitasker, and that applies to listening too. So, when it's time to talk, I know that my phone needs to be face down and my laptop needs to be closed. Even the ringing sound of an incoming text message or email will distract me, and I will miss something important that she said.

If you are passionate about getting your point across in a conversation, how do you do that while also ensuring that you're respecting the thoughts and opinions of others?

Remove distractions - as in my prior example, many of us get distracted easily during conversations. We may be preoccupied with something else and quickly discover that we can't pay full attention to someone. Or, for my fellow overthinkers, someone may be talking, but our mind begins to wander.

During our conversation, they said something that triggered a thought; now, our thoughts have drifted to another path, and we're no longer fully attentive to them. Whatever it may be, identify the things that can get your attention and work to remove them while someone else is talking, even if only for a few minutes.

Write down your point - a common reason that some people may interrupt or want to jump in quickly during a discussion is that they're afraid of forgetting a thought. This is why it's always good to be prepared to take notes.

When someone is speaking, and a thought hits you, write that thought down on a piece of paper or type it into your phone (note – it's good practice to let the person know you'll be doing that, so they don't take your writing as you not paying attention). When the opportunity presents itself to jump into the conversation and share, you'll now have notes to refer to.

Plan Of Action

Repeat something they said – listening is one thing, but being engaged is entirely different. You can tell when someone is involved in what you're saying. One thing that I look to do when discussing a topic with me is repeat something they said. Imagine a coworker is talking to you about a report that they have been working on that is due this week.

After discussing it with you for a few minutes, you respond and say:

"Interesting, I like your approach (insert interesting point they made). Great job."

 Not only does that signal to the person that you were listening, but it signals that you cared about what they had to say. This builds trust and loyalty with people as they realize you genuinely desire to hear and understand them.

Don't multitask - does multitasking work? Based on studies referenced by the Cleveland Clinic, multitasking hinders most people's performance. This is because multitasking divides the brain's attention, making us less efficient [14]. This same thing applies to listening. Stay focused in a meeting or in the middle of a discussion.

The goal is to retain as much information as possible, which becomes complicated when our attention is split.

Make eye contact – consider for a moment how you feel when you're talking to someone and they're looking at their phone. Or when you're speaking in a meeting, you glance across the room and see someone chatting with the person next to them.

Those are typically indications of people not engaging in the conversation. When you intentionally make eye contact with the person speaking, it becomes a forcing function for you to listen. It also signals to the person speaking that you are with them.

SHOW EMPATHY

"In a world where we appear to be more desensitized from the human experience than ever, it is more important than ever that we learn to become more empathic."

One Sunday morning, on June 18th, 2023, a submarine with five passengers boarded a voyage to see the site of the Titanic crash. By the next day, news broke worldwide that the submarine had disappeared. A search and rescue mission was launched and continued over the following days. I recall waking up on the morning of June 22nd, 2023, and seeing news headlines stating that the remains from the submarine had been found at the bottom of the ocean, confirming everyone's worst fears about the fate of the passengers onboard [15]. Something that I found extremely disturbing throughout this drama was the reaction to it on social media. During the submarine's disappearance, several memes and jokes were flying around. Some people commented on how they would never have gotten on a submarine like that; others said they would have never paid that much to see the Titanic, and in some cases, people were in comments simply leaving laughing emojis.

The more posts I saw about it, with people mocking a tragedy, the more I wondered if I was somehow the outsider. How is it possible that our world has become so cold? When did it become okay to laugh at death? How is it possible that we've become a society of little to no empathy?

In today's world, we all see and hear disturbing news. The fatal shooting in a local neighborhood, the terrorist attack, the alert letting us know that a child has gone missing, and the report detailing the number of lives lost in a war. We hear about it, feel sorry for that day (sometimes a few seconds), then move on to the next story in the news cycle. In a world where we appear to be more desensitized from the human experience than ever before, it is more important than ever that we learn to become more empathic.

The word empath is defined as:

"Being one who is capable of experiencing the emotions of others" [16]

In an article from Psychology Today, author and UCLA professor Judith Orloff makes the point that both introverts and extroverts can be empaths and describes the experiences of being on either side [17]. Regardless of a person's personality and general demeanor, there is an innate human ability to feel someone, though it may be at different levels for some of us.

Ultimately, we can have all the degrees, training, personal development, and self-help that money can buy. But if we can remember one fundamental kindergarten principle, we can relate and connect with people.

The golden rule is to treat others how you would like to be treated.

Feeling cared for, thought about, and seen creates a more open and relaxed environment. Environments like this encourage people to feel comfortable, calm and want to stay.

PLAN OF ACTION

Walk in their shoes — the pastor of my church has used an example in the past of 'getting in the well' with someone. In the example, he communicates that one of the most effective ways to support a struggling friend is to be with them and listen. Not trying to fix things, not condemning them for their situation, but just being an ear, being a shoulder to cry on. This is what empathy should look like. When you know someone you work with is having a hard time, figure out how you can be there for them. Maybe it's taking them to lunch one day and letting them vent; maybe it's asking them (genuinely) how things are going and taking the time to hear the answer. Be willing to get in the well.

Check-in frequently - according to the US census in 2021, around 3.4 million people died, or over 9,300 people per day [18]. In death, loved ones are left going through immense grief and heartbreak. If you're reading this, there's a good chance you've lost someone you loved closely at some point. I know that I have. When people attend a funeral or send messages like – "I'm sorry for your loss" or "I offer my condolences," it often comes from a heartfelt place with good intentions. Unfortunately, weeks go by after the funeral, and the messages stop.

The family is now left to go through that grief alone. A part of showing empathy is consistency in our help and concern for people. If someone that you work with is struggling in an area or is trying to come up to speed on a task, don't just check in on them once. Make it a consistent habit to see how they're progressing.

ESTABLISH YOUR CORE THREE

"To remain calm and to keep a level head, sometimes we must have someone else to express our thoughts and feelings to."

The number of people willing to share their business on social media always amazes me. People will do everything from complain about their spouse to talk bad about their job to threaten violence against people on a completely public social platform.

A reason why people love to post on social media is due to dopamine. People get a high when they post a video, a picture, or a caption, and people like it. However, it's a lot deeper than that.

A lot of people don't have anyone to talk to. Granted, they may have some people they occasionally socialize with or even socialize with often. But who do they go to when they have a problem? Who do they go to when they just had a terrible day at work, their business isn't growing, or their relationship is in shambles? For people who don't have anyone, many seek to capture attention through various avenues. But there are three types of people that everyone should have: a core three that help to bring stability and a sense of community that will help you. For any introvert reading this, although you likely value your alone time, having these core three in place can help take things to the next level.

Although in this book, we're primarily focusing on reaching our full potential by operating in calmness, there will undoubtedly be circumstances that will upset you. Additionally, walking in calm confidence does not mean you'll be immune to trouble and never get frustrated. I can recall times when my coworkers or business partners assumed everything with me was going perfectly fine; on the outside, I'm sure it appeared that way. But internally, I was going through a battle they did not know about. Some situations can even push you to want to do something drastic.

In these moments of frustration, having people with your best interests in mind is critical.

So why is this important?

1) It can keep us from doing something that we shouldn't. Let's be honest: for many of us, our most embarrassing moments have come when we first said or did something without wise advice.

2) In the heat of our emotions, all we can see is our problem. But often, someone else can come into that same situation from the outside looking in, hear us, and offer an entirely different perspective. That perspective alone and us just talking it out can make a huge difference.

Your core three consists of the people described in this chapter's action plan. As an exercise from this chapter, write out who you believe your core three to be. If you don't have names identified, that's okay. Commit to finding them; your future self will thank you.

PLAN OF ACTION

The Confidant - every great leader needs somebody that they can confide in. A president has a vice president and a general counsel. A head coach has assistant coaches. Leaders should be operating in collaboration with others.

There are times when you'll have a rough day, times when you'll need advice, and other times when you'll need someone to vent to. Your confidant is there to help you to see things from a different perspective. To remain calm and to keep a level head, sometimes we must have someone else to express our thoughts and feelings to.

Find someone within your circle that you can trust with this responsibility.

The Mentor - If we're the most intelligent person in the room, it's time to graduate to another room. A mentor knows more than we do and has been where we're trying to go. They have already fought the battles we're fighting and came out on the other side. This person's role in your life is to share their past experiences with you, be an ear to hear you and provide guidance and suggestions. Picture a person that you admire. You could admire them for any number of reasons, but whatever it is, they have something that you respect and look up to. You want to model and absorb information from this type of person consistently.

The Advocate - a popular phrase states that it's not what you know, but who you know. For the first ten years of my career, if I wanted to look for a new job opportunity, my first instinct was to look up available jobs online, apply, and hope to hear back from a recruiter. These days, if I'm searching for an opportunity, I first reach out to people I know. One reason that forming relationships is so important is that you put yourself in a position to have an advocate. An advocate is someone who's going to fight for you, someone who is going to speak your praises when you're not in the room, and someone who has the potential to present you with new opportunities based on their impression and belief in your work ethic. Having this one person as part of your core three can transform your career or your business. However, not having this person makes it much harder to progress.

ACKNOWLEDGE OTHER PERSPECTIVES

"In our self-absorbed world dominated by selfies, people in search of likes, people in search of followers, and people that focus on their opinion, you will set yourself apart by being able to understand and walk in someone else's shoes."

Spending time with my family is one of my favorite things to do; that completely takes my mind away from work.

And if I'm honest, sometimes I've dropped the ball in this area. Here's a typical scene in our house. I'm sitting at the desk in my office with three computer screens going, typing away rapidly while thinking about whatever I'm writing. I hear the sliding door to my office slowly opening, and when I look up, I see my 8-year-old son Amari. He'll walk over to me and usually say something like:

"Hey, Daddy, can we play?"

In most cases, I'm working on something that must get done; most likely, it's a task tied to a deadline that I have to meet. I'll find myself explaining how Daddy has to get some work done first; I then promise to come into his room as soon as I'm done. That response is usually met with a conversation that turns into a negotiation.

"Well, how long do you have to work, Daddy? 10 minutes? Can you be done in 5 minutes?"

Other times, my response is met with a reaction that hits me in the gut.

I'll say that I must get some work done, and I can visually look at his face and see his disappointment. With his head down, he starts walking toward the door to leave. I used to not notice it as much, but I do now. Consequently, I've been making an effort (not 100% of the time, but doing better) to stop whatever I'm doing workwise in those moments to come to play with him, even if only for a short time. From his perspective, he has come home from school and wants to spend time with his dad. I understand this feeling because I felt the same about my dad growing up.

When I tell him about the work that I have to do, he hears that my work is more important than our time together. It took me a while to understand this. Additionally, I know a day will come when he'll be quicker to call his friends to hang out than to come looking for me. For that reason, I must treasure our time together and embrace our bonding time. The ability to see the world from another person's eyes is rare, mainly because most humans are self-absorbed. But doing this allows us to relate, feel, and bond with others.

Understanding varying perspectives of thought is a skill that comes naturally for most introverts without realizing it. Although many people in society would believe that to be untrue. The commonly held myth that introverts are somehow antisocial or socially withdrawn can lead to thoughts that introverts want nothing to do with people. They often take the fact that an introvert enjoys time alone or the fact that an introvert doesn't always want to be in a crowd to mean one or both of the following:

1. They need to gain social skills.

2. They don't enjoy socializing.

Therefore, with that theory in mind, how can an introvert relate, understand, and socialize with someone with an extroverted personality, especially in a professional environment? Not only are these myths and lies untrue, but in many cases, it's the complete opposite. Research and human psychology have shown no evidence of links between introversion and someone's ability to socialize. It just simply isn't true. However, what is true is that many introverts enjoy deep and meaningful conversations.

When talking to someone, there is a connection that the introvert enjoys, a connection that may only be experienced with a few people. For those that an introvert desires to connect with, they are likely to experience the following:

- Someone who genuinely listens to them.
- Someone who tends to think deeply about what's being said to them.
- Someone who can genuinely absorb that person's thoughts and feelings.

Do any of the above three traits describe you? People with these traits can connect and see where others are coming from. In our self-absorbed world dominated by selfies, people in search of likes and followers, and people who focus on their opinions, you will set yourself apart by being able to understand and walk in someone else's shoes.

Plan Of Action

Know what motivates someone. Throughout my career, I've worked with countless veterans across all branches of the United States military.

One thing that has kept me motivated is knowing that the programs I've worked on all had an underlying mission. In many of those programs, the products that we helped to deliver played a role in saving lives. But for the former servicemen and women I've had the pleasure of working with, the meaning of the work is entirely different. I've had coworkers tell me stories of eating dinner with their best friend one night and finding out the next day that friend had been killed. I've also heard stories where a particular technology delivered by our company protected someone from becoming a casualty of war and unable to return home to their family. My view of the importance of what I do pales in comparison to my coworkers who have lived it.

What motivates the people around you? What is their backstory? The more you get to know about those around you, the better you'll be able to relate to them. It can start with simple one-on-one conversations; it doesn't have to be formal. But find time to figure out a person's motivations, desires, dislikes, and passions.

Eliminate bias – sometimes, we can introduce our personal bias without realizing it. I'm going to be honest: I've made this mistake with several extroverts. For example, I would observe a person's personality in a meeting setting where they came off as somewhat brash, loud, or boisterous. Seeing that, I assumed that person and I would have little in common. But truthfully, I have been wrong about this on so many occasions. Some of the same people I viewed that way turned into great working relationships. So, be careful not to approach relationships with preconceived notions. People might surprise you.

PART V - RELAXATION

"The same way that a battery needs to be put on a charger when it runs low, the introvert needs rest to recharge and attack the day."

I grew up seeing both of my parents work a lot. As an accountant, my dad traveled frequently and, when in town, would often work long days, leading to him coming home late in the evening. As a teacher, my mother would work in classrooms full of kids all day, come home, and then run my sister and me back and forth to our various extracurricular activities. Both were highly dedicated to their faith, family, and professions. One day, while I was back home from college, my dad, mom, sister, and I enjoyed a semi-pro football game at American Airlines Center in downtown Dallas.

At one point during the game, in between the four of us laughing and talking, my dad leaned over to me and said:

"See.... this is what it's all about. No money can buy days like this."

I didn't understand what he was trying to tell me then, but now I do. No matter how hard you work and how much money is in your bank account, it's more important to embrace moments. Our moments are not infinite; one day, they will expire. So, what do we want to be known for when that day comes? You should ponder that question as you read through the rest of this chapter.

Rest is vital for our spirit, mind, and body. It forces us to break away from the daily grind of life and create moments of calm that are meaningful to us.

Our society has become more and more addicted to work. While some people strive to achieve work-life balance, that balance has become an illusion for many. You can even hear the addiction to working in our language.

Casual statements made between coworkers about the mountain of emails they expect to come back to after taking time off for a week. Or the person who takes time off but sends a message to their team saying:

"If anything urgent comes up, I can be reached at (insert phone number)."

Let me go ahead and throw myself into this. Last year, on a family road trip, we left Dallas on a journey that would take us across six states in a week. During the first few days of the trip, I frequently pulled out my work phone to see if I had any urgent missed calls or voicemails. With all the critical activities going on that week at the office, I was on edge about taking off that week. Eventually, a look from my wife while reaching for my phone (to say a look of disgust would be putting it lightly) led me to put my phone in my bag and leave it there until we returned home from the trip. And I'm glad that I did.

Just look at some of these statistics collected in a blog post by Team Stage titled "Is There A Cost To Work Promotion in 2024?"

- 66% of full-time employees in America do not have a work-life balance.
- Spending more than 55 hours a week at work increases the risk of anxiety and depression.
- 40% of employees use their devices for work outside business hours [19].

Reading statistics like these, it becomes clear that many of us have completely forgotten what it means to rest.

Some people hear statistics like that and immediately begin thinking.

"Well, that's why I'm going to work for myself and be my boss!"

I hate to break the news to you, but that likely means you'll be working just as much, if not more. According to a survey by Inc. com [20]:

- 33% of small business owners said they work over 50 hours weekly.
- an additional 25% stated that they work more than 60 hours per week.

Sadly, the desire for freedom that attracts many people to entrepreneurship requires more time to keep a small business thriving. So what's the answer? How is it possible to have balance when you have a career, a family, social and extracurricular obligations? Or what about someone who may not have a significant other or children but still feels overwhelmed by everything life throws at them?

Well, a few years ago, when I expressed to my therapist how overwhelmed I was feeling at the time with working to prioritize my spiritual life, spending time with my family, publishing my first book, and working in a full-time career, he taught me something that I'd like to share with you.

See, the truth is you may always find achieving balance to be challenging. In some cases, balance may not exist this season, and being overwhelmed will be your reality. However, even amid that, you can choose to rest. See, here's what nobody tells you:

Prioritizing rest is your responsibility.

The same way that logging in for a meeting is, the same way that taking the kids to school is, or the same way that paying a bill is. Nobody else will make it essential except you. The good news is that a fantastic thing happens when you make it a point to find time to rest your mind, body, and spirit.

It is easier to operate in a space of calm and peace of mind. For introverts who require time to recharge, that time allows us to operate at maximum potential and becomes even more critical. It is difficult to operate at our full capacity when we're constantly on the go, around people, or distracted. In this final key of the calm effect, we'll explore principles that will help you to relax and recharge. In the same way that a battery must be put on a charger when it runs low, the introvert needs rest to recharge, remain calm and attack the day.

UNPLUG

"To unplug means that we get a chance to declutter the thousands of thoughts we have each day, evaluate our current mental state, and assess how life is going."

If you work in the corporate world or own a business, then there is a good chance that you have an addiction. You most likely don't realize that an addiction exists because your daily routine seems normal to you. Due to your drive to be successful, or what society would consider to be success, you continue to operate at the level that you do. But what if I told you that your addiction can become dangerous? The addiction is busyness, an inability to relax and unplug. By the way, I'm an addict too.

Many of us wake up in the morning, and one of the first things on our minds is what we must get done throughout the day. After hitting the snooze button a few times and getting ready, our minds go directly into work mode. For entrepreneurs, social media would lead you to envision the life of a businessman or businesswoman sitting by the pool, drinking margaritas all day with their feet kicked up. Of course, the picture that no one seems to show is the entrepreneur who wakes up early, goes to bed late, and works seven days a week to grow their business.

Now I know what you may be thinking: what's the alternative? You must work if you have responsibilities, bills, and short-term and long-term goals.

Besides, choosing not to do so would make one irresponsible, uninspired, or lazy, right?

Now granted, some people refuse to work, and some people go through life wasting their potential. That is a genuine thing. But for the people who are addicted to busyness like me, where is the line between working toward your goals and making time to unplug for your spiritual, physical, and mental health? That's what we'll be exploring in this chapter.

I want you to ask yourself this fundamental question:

Do you spend more time giving to other people than you do to yourself?

Let me paint a scenario for you. A married woman of 12 years has a steady career, a loving relationship, three kids, and a life full of responsibilities. Her typical day consists of working, running errands, taking the kids to practice, cooking for the family, and finding time to sleep somewhere in between. Typically, she'll take two vacations a year with the family that she desperately looks forward to. On the last day of the vacation, on the flight or the car ride back home, she begins to feel sadness as she thinks about returning to her daily routine within 24 hours. All that she knows is that, for some reason, she feels tired and drained of energy most days.

Let's take a single male who has been steadily climbing the corporate ladder, working hard, and getting promoted. He is passionate about taking his career to the next level, so he spends much time working. In his mind, the only way to excel is to put in the necessary hours and to go above what is required. With that mindset, he finds himself regularly logging in to work late into the evening and missing out on quality time with his friends while believing that one day, it will all be worth it. Though he has no problem doing the work, he feels something is missing. He can't quite figure out what it is, but it's there. He is ambitious but feels empty inside.

These scenarios are more common than you may realize. Our addiction to staying busy and our desire to achieve can cause us to forget how to rest completely, leading us quickly to burn out. I can recall seasons in my career when I felt like I had nothing left to give and times when my gas tank was empty. Have you ever had that feeling? It can be pretty scary. To know that something is wrong but not know what it is. To feel helpless, exhausted, and emotionally spent. That's what burnout can feel like.

The good news is that if we can break away from our daily routines, worries, and stresses, it helps to reset the mind. To unplug means that we can declutter the thousands of thoughts each day, evaluate our current mental state, and assess how life is going. To operate with a sense of calm, we must learn how to manage our busy lifestyles while taking time for self-care.

PLAN OF ACTION

Take breaks - I love doing something simple on days I work from home and have spent 5 hours straight dialed into virtual meetings. I go for a walk to the mailbox. In our neighborhood, the mailbox is about two blocks away, but during my two-block walk, I get to take in some fresh air, feel the wind blow, observe the birds as they fly by, and decompress for a few minutes. Now, I know you may be thinking:

"A walk to the mailbox Terrance...seriously?"

You'd be surprised what a five-minute microbreak does for me mentally. Think about some mini breaks that you can implement throughout your day.

It could be participating in a short activity that you enjoy, it could be taking a walk, or it could be sitting somewhere and doing absolutely nothing. Whatever it is, figure that out and turn it into a consistent habit.

Have a self-care routine - sometimes in life, we can spend so much time giving to other people that we forget to give to ourselves. Again, going back to the earlier question:

Do you spend more time giving to other people than you do to yourself?

We give to our careers, we give to our businesses, we give to our families, we give to organizations.

But how often do we give to ourselves?

Come up with three activities that you love to do. In the same way you schedule time for your work and take care of your daily responsibilities, schedule time to do these three things every week. No matter how busy life gets, even if you must reduce the time you spend enjoying the three activities, put them on your calendar and commit to doing them.

A GREAT TEAM

"The key is to know what you're good at, and for everything else, identify someone that can help you."

My first rock climbing experience was in Denver, Colorado. It was indoor rock climbing, not climbing in the actual mountains like some daredevils that climb with chalk on their hands, jumping from rock to rock, hanging on for dear life. It wasn't quite that extreme. Even still, my first-time rock climbing was a little nerve-racking. The walls went up to the ceiling, roughly 50 feet high.

Although there were harnesses, foam mats on the ground, and other safety measures in place, my first thought was:

"Yeah, so, what are the chances of me falling?"

I got into the harness and began to climb the mountain slowly. With each step increasing, I would glance down at the ground, realizing how high I was. When I reached the top, fear set in. The instructor yelled:

"Now let go!"

This wasn't a surprise since the instructor had gone through this with me before climbing, but I paused for a second now that it was time to release.

Eventually, clutching onto the rope with both hands, I slowly let go and began heading toward the ground. After that, the next several climbs were easy. The more I climbed, the more confidence I had, knowing I had a harness and safety gear to hold me up.

Imagine if I had started climbing the wall for the first time with no harness. The responsibility was entirely on me to ensure that a foot or a hand didn't slip, causing me to fall rapidly toward the ground. It is not as comfortable of a feeling, for sure. That's the difference between doing things alone and having an excellent team to back you up.

Working alone may feel like we're in control, and it may even provide us with a level of comfort because it is what we're used to. However, when everything depends on one person's efforts, it will be difficult for that person to rest and function calmly.

There's something about knowing that you have good people on your side. It's like knowing that the school bully will be waiting for you after school when the bell rings, but also knowing that your big brother or sister will be standing next to you. When we're by ourselves, it typically makes things more challenging. For the introvert, this becomes a complicated paradox.

While breaking away from people allows us to recharge, it can also lead to a habit of trying to take on the world by oneself. Instead of asking for help or building a solid team, the natural reaction may be to work to increase individual skills and build on individual experiences.

Often, when people look at highly successful people juggling several different endeavors, they ask how it's possible. How can one person get so many things done? Almost always, the answer is that the person has a phenomenal team in place.

The truth is that having a team opens more possibilities for you to rest. When you are the one who thinks of every idea, creates everything, executes everything, and follows up on everything, it becomes draining and exhausting.

Unfortunately, this is often a recipe that leads to anxiety.

Now close your eyes and picture this. You look up one day and realize that other people are now handling 50% of the tasks that used to keep you stressed out. How would that feel? As I've been implementing this practice within my role, it's been freeing. One straightforward step you can take is to write a list of all the current tasks you're responsible for completing. Whether the task is minor or significant, write them down. Now, I want you to divide the tasks into two categories:

Category 1 – tasks that only you can get done.

Category 2 – tasks that can be done by someone else.

That may seem overly simplified, but most people never do this. We go through our days working, thinking we're being productive, but a lot of the things we're doing could've been handled by someone else. We need to take this step to be able to handle our workload. So the next time you're working on something, ask the question:

"Am I the one that has to be doing this?"

In the beginning, you may be worried about letting go of your work. You might have thought you were the only person who could do it at a high level and do it with your level of intention. But after doing this exercise, you may look up and realize just how much time you've been wasting. That wasted time can now be allocated to other things, which automatically benefits you and your well-being. I bet you feel better just thinking about it; I know I did. Remember, it's much less stressful to climb when you've got a harness. So, the question becomes, how do you find people that can help you? Next, we'll talk about the kind of people that you should look for.

Plan Of Action

Find someone whose strengths are your weaknesses — I love writing; it is one of the most fulfilling activities I'm blessed to do.

But if you asked me to design a book cover, I would need to figure out where to start, and I'm sure whatever I designed would not make you a bestseller! So, I hire a graphic designer for my book covers. My designer gets to operate in his zone of genius, and I sit back calmly, knowing that an amazing design is coming my way.

The key is knowing the tasks you excel at and identifying someone who can do the other tasks better.

Find someone reliable — Think about the people that you work with or interact with regularly. Would you consider them to be reliable? After being around someone for extended periods, you notice patterns. Those patterns may be admirable, or they may be destructive. When you know someone you trust to get a job done, be willing to give them some of your responsibilities. It will allow them to work on something new and allow you to decrease your workload.

MOMENTS OF SOLITUDE

"Sometimes being alone can be what we need to rest our mind, spark ideas, and function at our highest capacity."

Throughout history, people have detached from society to be alone to concentrate on their craft. Creatives such as musicians and artists retreat to locations where they can be completely isolated to focus on their work. In 2020, Hollywood mogul Tyler Perry, known for producing and directing countless television shows and movies through his company Tyler Perry Studios, revealed that he writes all his shows himself [21]. Given the amount of content that Tyler produces, this came as a shock to most people, as the typical television show would be created in a room full of writers. But Tyler can be alone, think, and create content that is watched in millions of homes.

Steve Wozniak, cofounder of one of the largest companies in the world, is credited with designing the hardware that became the Apple 1, Apple's first computer. In speaking on productivity and work environment, Steve has offered the following quote:

"I don't believe anything revolutionary has ever been invented by committee... I'm going to give you some advice that might be hard to take. That advice is: Work alone... Not on a committee. Not on a team." ~ Steve Wozniak

Interestingly, one of the factors that contributed to Apple's success was the pairing of Steve with the extroverted Steve Jobs. While Steve W. could quietly innovate, Steve J. became the company's visionary and the ultimate salesman. This partnership proved to be legendary, and incredibly profitable.

On the far end of the spectrum, we can examine the life of a monk. Monks typically vow poverty, celibacy, and extreme obedience while agreeing to live alone or within a community of other monks. They live a life that is separated from society, allowing them the space and solitude to be dedicated to their religion.

The desire for solitude can be misunderstood in a society that often encourages group work and group interaction. However, for so many people, particularly introverts, sometimes being alone can be exactly what we need to rest our minds, spark ideas, and function at our highest capacity.

The human brain processes thousands of thoughts per day. These thoughts can relate to everything from repetitive tasks that are part of our daily routine, to major decisions we need to make, a recent encounter with a friend or family member, or anything in between. When we think about solitude, it can become a layered topic. As human beings, we are innately social creatures. At some level, we all desire human connection; in the right circumstances, that connection is healthy for us. The ability to talk about what you're going through at work with a significant other or a friend, the beautiful laughter of one of your kids when you all are playing together, or the hug you get from a family member you haven't seen in years. These are precious experiences that money can't buy.

At the same time, spending time alone is essential as well. If you consider yourself an introvert, the need for solitude becomes even more critical. After socializing for extended periods, whether throughout your workday or personal life, you look forward to enjoying downtime where you can recharge and refocus. Being forced to socialize without breaks can become draining because an introvert gains energy through alone time. This becomes extremely important to understand and is where self-awareness is critical.

For example, if you're leading a team and the environment is one where you're around fellow teammates for several hours nonstop, you should assess how you feel throughout that time. Some introverts can hit a wall, a wall where the desire to be social fades, and the desire to leave sets in. This often has nothing to do (most times) with how the introvert feels about the group but is more driven by the introvert's social battery. Unfortunately, some people would mistake this for being antisocial or rude, but that couldn't be farther from the truth. If you realize you operate better professionally and personally after time alone, take the necessary time. I will tell you that during my writing process of creating *Quiet Voice Fearless Leader* and now *The Calm Effect*, I routinely went through long periods where I didn't interact with anyone. Just me in a room with a laptop, cell phone off, no television, no distractions.

Sometimes, that's what it takes to clear our minds, detach, and create an atmosphere that allows us to think.

PLAN OF ACTION

Don't feel guilty - have you ever agreed to go somewhere when you knew you didn't feel like it? After socializing all week, you've decided to hang out with friends or coworkers one evening but realize your energy is completely tapped. All you want to do now is relax and enjoy some time alone at home. In these moments, if you don't feel like going to a function, I want you not to feel guilty about not going. I'm not saying to be rude or dismissive toward the person who invited you. I'm also not saying that you should never go.

Both actions can have negative consequences for your relationships if not handled tactfully. But it's essential to avoid guilting yourself into attending events when you need solitude to recharge your social battery.

Don't isolate - while solitude is essential for introverts, there is another side. There's a fine line between solitude and isolation. Solitude means taking temporary time to oneself for rest, reflection, enjoying a hobby, or anything else that restores and brings an individual peace of mind. In contrast, isolation is a concerted effort to avoid the outside world for extended amounts of time. Isolation can be dangerous for many reasons. When we isolate, we remove ourselves from the ability to make human connections, don't share or express our feelings with other people, and begin to hold things in. If we're not careful, this way of thinking can make us feel lonely, uncared for, and disconnected. I know because I've been there. So, while our solitude is beneficial, ensure you don't cross the line from solitude to complete isolation.

YOU'RE NOT IN CONTROL

"Enjoy what you can and ignore the rest. Let's not waste any energy fighting things outside our control." ~Paulo Coelho

Within a few months of my daughter being born, we had to take her to the hospital due to complications with breathing. She had already proven herself a fighter on the day of her birth. As my wife was pushing feverishly during labor, with no medication I might add, our daughter's head got stuck on my wife's pelvic bone. After continuing to push through excruciating pain, my wife gave birth to our daughter Aminah. The struggle to come out had caused Aminah to have busted blood vessels in both of her eyes and several bruises on her face. Nevertheless, she was placed in my wife's arms shortly after, then into mine, and as she looked up at me, our eyes connected. It was a feeling I will never forget.

A few months later, my wife and I noticed a wheezing noise whenever Aminah breathed. At first, you could barely even hear it, but as the days continued, it got louder. Finally, after trying several medications and home remedies, we decided to take her to the doctor. We arrived at the emergency room one afternoon for what we thought would be a routine appointment. That appointment ended up turning into a four-day stay in the hospital.

After hours of tests, nurses, and doctors coming in and out of the room, my wife and I were eventually told that she had developed a rare breathing condition. For the next several days, she was hooked up to a machine to assist her with breathing as we sat by her bedside. Every minute in that room felt like an eternity. I sat there, a father wanting to be a protector, a father wanting to make everything okay, a father with tears in my eyes every day, realizing that I was utterly powerless. All I wanted was for my little girl to be able to breathe.

In the grand scheme of things, a lot of the issues that we deal with from day to day don't matter. As humans, we worry about everything.

How are things going at work?

Will our business be successful?

Is our current relationship going to work out?

How are we going to get everything done on our to-do list?

Are people going to like and accept us?

Not many things are certain in this life, but there's one that is. That one thing is change; usually, it happens when you least expect it. Even as I'm writing this, I recently discovered that my desktop computer, which I use for much of my writing and video editing, was no longer booting up. The other morning, after getting out of the shower and walking to my sink to shave, the hair clippers that I usually use were no longer working. There's no way I could've predicted either of these things would happen, and there's no way you'll be able to predict every moment of your day. But that's life. Extraordinarily, realizing that you are not in control gives you a sense of peace.

The reality is that all the spreadsheets, to-do lists, and organizational apps on your phone do not mean you're in control. Don't get me wrong, there's nothing wrong with organization, and there's nothing wrong with planning. As the saying goes, if you fail to plan, then you plan to fail.

However, how do you react when your plans don't come to fruition as you thought they would?

Some common reactions might include fear, anger, doubt, worry, sadness, and maybe even depression. But it's in these exact moments that remembering the calm effect can help you. Stop and think to yourself:

"Well...I didn't see that coming!"

Take about 30 seconds to breathe, think of a funny thought that will make you laugh, calm your nerves, and move along with the day.

Problems will occur, and you will have to adjust. It's just life. So, in those moments, relax, breathe, and be calm.

PLAN OF ACTION

Practice letting go - as introverts; our minds can quickly lead us down a path of overthinking. The way we wish a meeting or conversation had gone or the point we wanted to make but decided to keep it to ourselves instead. Well, despite our immediate regret during those times, until we leave this earth, there will always be a tomorrow. So, when a meeting doesn't go well, when we bomb our presentation, or when we receive negative feedback from someone on our performance, it may feel like the end of the world, but it's not. There will be a tomorrow, so don't let your mind overthink yesterday. Learn to let go and keep fighting.

Control what you can - once we can let go of past mistakes and learn to avoid excessive worrying, we can now focus on perfecting the things we can control. We can control the level of effort given toward completing a task, our integrity when dealing with coworkers or business partners, and our attention to detail when putting together a presentation or a pitch. As already stated, life is unpredictable and full of surprises, so take care of the things you can control.

CONCLUSION

Recently, I gave a presentation at work and completely bombed it. You know those meetings where you feel like you have everything under control, you've gone over your presentation material countless times, rehearsed how to answer various questions, and generally feel prepared. Well, I went into the meeting feeling that way, and within five minutes, things quickly started to unravel. Errors in my data were pointed out that I should've caught, and questions I hadn't thought about were asked. After receiving a significant number of actions to follow up on and less than 24 hours to address them, I arrived home exhausted after a difficult day. After pulling my car into the garage and sitting in the car for a minute, I breathed a deep sigh.

Then, as soon as I opened the door to walk inside, I heard an angelic sound.

"Daddy!! Daddy!!"

My five-year-old daughter ran, jumped up, and embraced me in a full sprint. Looking at her gorgeous smile from ear to ear, I smiled back, and we continued to hug.

Instantly, I completely forgot about the presentation, the amount of work I had to get done that night, and how tired I felt. The warming spirit of a child had calmed my anxiety and fatigue.

I say that story for this reason. When we stop to remember what's important in our lives, walking in calmness is much easier. As a 43-year-old man who's seen many highs and lows, I've learned to trust in my faith and my family. I can work as hard as possible, put in countless hours at the office, write several books and pursue all the goals that my heart desires. And guess what, after all that work, I'll be gone one day. When that day comes, what will people say about me?

What will I be remembered for? I would genuinely hope that I'm remembered for more than my work. It's not that my work is insignificant, but life is so much more than that. When I finally realized what matters to me, my faith in Christ that my parents instilled in me, and my family, I achieved a level of calm that I couldn't explain or describe. Things that would have destroyed me years ago just don't matter as much anymore. I have my faults, doubts, and struggles, like everyone else. I'm still a work in progress and probably always will be, but I love the journey.

Here's a simple exercise that may help to put things in perspective for you. The truth is, regardless of what field or industry you're in, some days you are going to feel frustrated, uneasy or overwhelmed. On those days, it may be very tempting to give up, or to succumb to the pressure. So, when those days come, remember to ask yourself these questions:

What's important to me?

What do I want to be remembered for?

What will my legacy be?

Remembering the answers to these questions will help to keep you grounded and centered. For many of us, it is easy to lose sight of what's important, especially with the rapid pace of life. But when you remove the distractions, and remain focused on what matters, your ability to walk in calmness will increase.

In this book, we focused on five keys for mastering the art of intentional calmness. On the other side of the coin is an area where many people, both introverts and extroverts, struggle. If I'm being honest, I struggled with it for decades. To embrace the calm effect without embracing the other side is like driving a car, only pressing the brakes and never pressing the gas. Sometimes, there is a feeling in our stomach when we know we should've spoken up during a discussion, but we choose to stay quiet. A feeling when we had a great idea that we wanted to present, but an internal voice talked us out of it. A feeling when we know that we should assert ourselves, but instead we choose to stand down.

In the final book of The Introvert Leader series, *The Fire Effect*, we will explore the other side of the human dynamic, where we discover how to grow in our assertiveness and lead with authority. The goal is to build further on the core leadership principles for introverts presented in *Quiet Voice Fearless Leader* and the keys for intentional calmness that you've learned through *The Calm Effect*. To begin the final phase on your journey as an Introvert Leader, click on the QR code below:

Get Your Copy Of *The Fire Effect* Here:

I sincerely hope you gained value from reading this book and learned something that you can apply today. A reminder that the goal of this book and any other book in this series is not to change who you are at your core. The goal is for you to embrace your authentic self. The calm effect has been life-changing for me, and if you genuinely lean in, it can be life-changing for you as well. In conclusion, I'd like to leave you with this quote:

"Courage Is Grace Under Pressure"

~Ernest Hemingway

THANK YOU

I would sincerely like to thank you for taking the time to read *The Calm Effect*. There are millions of books to choose from, so I am incredibly humbled that you chose this one. I have one thing before you go. It's an opportunity to receive over 2 hours of coaching from me that goes beyond this book:

Boost Your Career With '*The Introvert Career Blueprint*'

THE INTROVERT CAREER BLUEPRINT

Discover the blueprint for excelling and advancing at work. I specifically developed the curriculum in this training for introverts who are looking to grow in their careers, without compromising who they are. Through this course, you will:

- Improve Your Job Search and Interview Skills
- Learn How To Be Seen In The Workplace
- Enhance Your Communication Skills
- Discover How To Get Promoted

and much more!

Scan below to access the blueprint today:

ACKNOWLEDGMENTS

I would like to thank my Lord and Savior, Jesus Christ, for being the ultimate example of calm, peace, patience and understanding.

REFERENCES

[1] - *Oxford Learner's Dictionaries,* Retrieved February 2024 from www.oxfordlearnersdictionaries.com/us/definition/american_english/calm_3#:~:text=noun-,noun,The%20police%20appealed%20for%20calm

[2] – "Extraversion and Introversion", *Psychologist World,* Retrieved February 2024 from https://www.psychologistworld.com/influence-personality/extraversion-introversion

[3] – Almond, Elliott, "49ers Defeat Bengals, 20-16, in Super Bowl", *Los Angeles Times,* Retrieved February 2024 from https://www.latimes.com/archives/la-xpm-1989-01-23-mn-671-story.html

[4] – Rodriguez, Tristi, "True story behind Montana's iconic 'John Candy' Super Bowl quip", *NBC Sports,* Retrieved February 2024 from https://www.nbcsportsbayarea.com/nfl/san-francisco-49ers/true-story-behind-montanas-iconic-john-candy-super-bowl-quip/1175255/

[5] - *Cambridge Dictionary,* Retrieved February 2024 from https://dictionary.cambridge.org/us/dictionary/english/poise

[6] – Marghzar, Dr. Sol, "The Science of Sound", *Stephen Arnold Music,* Retrieved February 2024 from https://stephenarnoldmusic.com/science-of-sound/

[7] – Kane, Paul, "'You lie' moment interrupting a presidential speech reflects the slide to disunity", *Washington Post,* Retrieved

February 2024 from https://www.washingtonpost.com/powerpost/you-lie-moment-interrupting-a-presidential-speech-reflects-the-slide-to-disunity/2019/02/04/5732cdca-28bb-11e9-984d-9b8fba003e81_story.html

(8) – "Energy Education", *University of Calgary,* Retrieved February 2024 from https://energyeducation.ca/encyclopedia/Law_of_conservation_of_energy

(9) – Schwarz, Joel, "Violence in the home leads to higher rates of childhood bullying", *University of Washington News,* Retrieved February 2024 from https://www.washington.edu/news/2006/09/12/violence-in-the-home-leads-to-higher-rates-of-childhood-bullying/

(10) – "The Cuban Missile Crisis", *Office Of The Historian,* Retrieved February 2024 from https://history.state.gov/milestones/1961-1968/cuban-missile-crisis

(11) "Average U.S. Adult Will Spend Equivalent of 44 Years of Their Life Staring at Screens: Poll", *People Magazine,* Retrieved February 2024 from https://people.com/human-interest/average-us-adult-screens-study/

(12) *Vocabulary.com,* Retrieved February 2024 from https://www.vocabulary.com/dictionary/understanding

(13) "How Much of Communication Is Nonverbal", *The University of Texas Permian Basin,* Retrieved February 2024 from https://online.utpb.edu/about-us/articles/communication/how-much-of-communication-is-nonverbal/

(14) – "Why Multitasking Doesn't Work", *Cleveland Clinic,* Retrieved February 2024 from https://health.clevelandclinic.org/science-clear-multitasking-doesnt-work

REFERENCES

(15) – Victor, Daniel, Jimenez, Jesus, Bogel-Burroughs, "Missing Titanic Submersible", *The New York Times*, Retrieved February 2024 from https://www.nytimes.com/live/2023/06/22/us/titanic-missing-submarine#:~:text=Pieces%20of%20the%20missing%20Titan,are%20with%20these%20five%20souls.

(16) *Merriam-Webster*, Retrieved February 2024 from https://www.merriam-webster.com/dictionary/empath

(17) – Orloff, Judith, "The Difference Between Introverted and Extroverted Empaths", *Psychology Today*, Retrieved February 2024 from https://www.psychologytoday.com/us/blog/the-empaths-survival-guide/202304/the-difference-between-introverted-and-extroverted-empaths

(18) – "Deaths and Mortality", *National Center for Health Statistics*, Retrieved February 2024 from https://www.cdc.gov/nchs/fastats/deaths.htm

(19) – "Work-Life Balance Stats: Is There a Cost to Work Promotion in 2024?", *TeamStage*, Retrieved February 2024 from https://teamstage.io/work-life-balance-stats/

(20) – Callahan, Ted, "Business Owners Work Twice as Much as Employees, Survey Finds, *Inc.com*, Retrieved February 2024 from https://www.inc.com/news/articles/200604/overworked.html

(21) – Bennett, Anita, "Tyler Perry Says He Writes All Of His Shows: "I Have No Writers Room"", *Deadline*, Retrieved February 2024 from https://deadline.com/2020/01/tyler-perry-writes-all-of-his-own-shows-1202822941/

Made in United States
Troutdale, OR
06/01/2024

20249249R00086